I didn't know that : from "ants in the pants
423 EVI   10978

P9-DTB-710

Evins, Karle...
Sheridan County Library

11-08

DEC 2 6 2008	**DATE DUE**	
MAR 3 1 2009		
MAY 2 1 2013		
MAR 0 1 2019		

I Didn't Know That

....

From "Ants in the Pants" to
"Wet Behind the Ears"—
The Unusual Origins of the Things We Say

....

Compiled and edited by

KARLEN EVINS

SHERIDAN COUNTY LIBRARY
100 West Laurel Ave.
Plentywood, MT 59254
406-765-2317

SCRIBNER

New York   London   Toronto   Sydney

SCRIBNER
1230 Avenue of the Americas
New York, NY 10020

Copyright © 2007 by Karlen Evins

All rights reserved, including the right of
reproduction in whole or in part in any form.

First Scribner trade paperback edition 2007

SCRIBNER and design are trademarks of
Macmillan Library Reference USA, Inc., used under license
by Simon & Schuster, the publisher of this work.

For information about special discounts for bulk purchases,
please contact Simon & Schuster Special Sales:
1-800-456-6798 or business@simonandschuster.com

Designed by Kyoko Watanabe
Text set in RotisSerif

Manufactured in the United States of America

7 9 10 8 6

Library of Congress Control Number: 2006052235

11.00 11/08

Ingram

10978

ISBN-13: 978-1-4165-3238-5
ISBN-10: 1-4165-3238-2

This book was previously published by the author in two separate volumes
entitled *I Didn't Know That, Vol. I* copyright © 1992 by Karlen Evins
and *I Didn't Know That, Vol. II* copyright © 1993 by Karlen Evins.

To Richard

. . . for teaching me to fly

Acknowledgments

IT'S BEEN fourteen years since I touched the files of this manuscript. (So long ago that finding someone who could crack the code of a SyQuest 88 megadisk was an "I didn't know that" unto itself.)

To those who helped in my early days of self-publishing— Bill Hudson, Susan Browne, Tom Wiley, and Andy Tolbird— a special thanks for all you did to get this project off the ground.

To those who have encouraged its renaissance—Susan Moldow, Samantha Martin, and Lisa Drew of Scribner— thank you for making my transition into the real world of publishing such a pleasurable one.

To my own home support team—Darcy Anderson and David Turner—thank you for keeping me sane and our business going in the course of the day-to-day.

To Richard Sutphen, for the encouragement, the friendship, and the gracious introductions.

To Richard and Sabyrna Bach, thank you for sharing your world with me.

And to my business partner, cohost, and mentor, Teddy Bart, *This one's for you!* Thank you for taking an untrained little girl fresh out of college and giving her the confidence, the opportunity, and the encouragement of ten thousand angels. Amazing what happens when given permission to try. Thank you for teaching me not only how to ask the questions, but more important, how to listen for the answers.

A Note from the Author
(or, The Story Behind the Stories . . .)

IN MY twenties I developed a hobby of collecting words, phrases, and expressions while I was learning the ropes of my radio career. With a god-child in England, and any excuse I could muster to peruse old book-stores here and abroad, I began collecting what was to me fascinating trivia that I soon learned livened up most any conversation.

No sooner had I entered the world of talk radio as a pro-ducer than I was asked to fill in on a morning talk show as the female on the panel. While terrified at the thought of speaking my mind with so little experience, I warmed instantly to the thought of sharing my findings, for they were always greeted with enthusiasm and laughter and quite often the response, "Well, I didn't know that!"

As anyone who has ever published a book knows, it only takes about three people telling you, "You should write a book!" for you to think it just might work. In my radio-producing spare time, I began laying out my expressions in the form of a simple little self-published work, and I sold a few copies from my garage. A couple of years and many broken fingernails later, I placed my cottage industry in the attic, as my radio career went to television, consuming more and more of my time.

Many moons later, while visiting with writer friends, discussing works far more worthy of our time, I left my little books behind as a thank-you gift for their hospitality. A couple of introductions later and *I Didn't Know That* found its way to the Big Apple, a far cry from where it began in my little home in Nashville, Tennessee.

Please note that at the time of the original manuscript, there was no Internet, no Googling, no Snopes to verify the stories. Truth be told, most expressions cannot be confirmed entirely, though I can tell you that those listed here were, at least to someone's way of thinking, expressed for the reasons so given.

Some expressions adapted new meanings as they were carried from culture to culture. Others were slurred into different words entirely as they evolved from their original structure. I have done my best to trace the expressions here to their earliest or most likely origins, but as some of the original expressions were handed down word-of-mouth, generation to generation . . . you can only imagine the challenges in verifying everything as fact.

This book was written in a spirit of love. The stories will make you smile; some will make you think. But if we've done our job, most will have you saying, "I didn't know that," before it's all said and done.

Introduction

IN COMPILING this book, I was reminded of a story my grandpa once told me about a young bride preparing her first Thanksgiving meal under the watchful eye of her new husband. When she got to the holiday ham, she systematically cut off the ends and placed it in a pan. Her new husband, not certain of the proper cooking procedure for hams, asked his bride, "Why did you cut off the ends?" Her reply: "Because my mother always did."

Later that day, the mother of the bride showed up early to help, and the newlywed husband thought it an opportune time to learn more about this strange family custom. So he pulled his new mother-in-law aside and asked, "It all makes sense; but why did she cut off the ends of the ham before cooking?" With as much consideration as the daughter had given the question earlier, the mother-in-law answered, "Because *my* mother always did."

Finally the meal was prepared, the guests were seated,

and in the mix of the conversation, the grandmother of the bride was posed the same question by a now most curious grandson-in-law. "Grandma, just one thing . . . why the end-trimming before you cook a ham?"

With aging hands, the grandmother held hers up, gesturing before him, and replied, "Well, in my day, the pans were only this big!"

The story makes a point, which is that our reasons for many of the things we do today make little sense logically, though at one time, perhaps they did.

Every expression we use today has a story. Each word comes to us from something that had meaning at the time. We need only listen to our colorful language for a few minutes to know that ours is a culture steeped in tradition.

And tradition is good! But tradition without meaning is like wasting the ends of a perfectly good ham.

If we choose to hold to traditions, then surely we owe them the respect of knowing their origins.

Here's hoping this book brings you as much laughter and enlightenment in the reading as it did for me in its preparation.

I Didn't
Know That

More than a steak sauce, the phrase itself connotes the very best, because, by definition, it was the highest rating that could be given a ship insured by Lloyd's of London. Lloyd's registry of ships and shipping was categorized by letter and number (with ships graded by letter, and cargo by number). "A" meant the ship itself was perfect, and "1" meant the cargo was in perfect condition.

Aftermath

While we all know that the aftermath of a situation pertains to the consequences, it is perhaps helpful to know what a math is, which those consequences follow! A math, in the olden days, was a mowing, or more specifically, a mowed crop of hay. The aftermath referred to a second crop of hay that came along after the mowing or the harvest, which gives us today's meaning of "a by-product that came about after the original action."

All Gussied Up

What is a gussy, anyway? Well, we're not sure, but we do know what a gusset is! A gusset is a piece of material, triangular in shape, inserted into a garment to enhance its fit and form. A person said to have gusseted her dress was simply improving her appearance; thus to be all gussied up meant to go all out (dresswise) for the occasion.

Amateur

From the Latin word *amator,* our word *amateur* translates "a lover." Today the word connotes one lacking the experience to be called a professional. But the original meaning dealt more with motive rather than ranking. The first amateur engaged in a pastime for the *love* of that pastime, as opposed to taking on the task for money. For the artist or the athlete today who truly loves the profession he's chosen, perhaps a "professional" amateur label would best apply.

Ambition

The word we use today to describe one's fervent desire to get somewhere came to us from the Latin word *ambitio*, which literally translates: "go getter." The first go-getters were ancient Romans . . . more specifically, Roman politicians, who were going to get votes. Because political recognition was something to be desired (especially if you were a commoner, aspiring for more than just the simple life), the *ambitio*s were those who sought fame and power by way of politics to better their own lots in life.

Ampersand (&)

Ever wonder about the little do-jiggy that looks like this—&? Derived from the Latin *et* as a shorthand version of *and*, the ampersand got its present name from early English schoolrooms. Upon reciting the alphabet, each letter was memorized "*a* per se *a*, *b* per se *b* . . ." and so on. Following each letter was the symbol &, memorized as "*and* per se *and*" . . . and that's why it's *ampersand* today.

(To Run) Amuck

This one we borrowed from the Malayans. When the natives of the Malay Peninsula first encountered the white man (i.e., the enemy), they became very excited and were quoted as yelling the phrase *"Amoq! Amoq!"* Interpreted, the words meant "Kill! Kill!" To run amuck, as we have carried the phrase over today, quite simply refers back to that image of native tribesmen, running wild and scared, wanting to kill their perceived enemies.

Ants in His Pants

Just the thought of it makes you squirm, doesn't it? Well, that was the idea! Ants in the pants was actually an old English folk remedy for "tired blood." In the late 1700s, the belief was that if someone slept more than his fair share, or was more lethargic than normal, an antidote was in order. To quicken circulation, one prescription of the day was to place ants in the pants of the patient. Not to be confused with having a "bee in one's bonnet"! (This one connotes a mental obsession, as when one can't get something out of one's mind.)

Apple Pie Order

Some say it has to do with the apples *in* the pies, others will tell you it has to do with the arrangement of apple pies *on* the shelf, but the bottom line is that the phrase "apple pie order" dates back to the days of the early pioneers, when wives of the frontiersmen did their baking at the first of the week. Arranging the apples within the pie, and arranging the pies on the shelves once they were cooked were both neat and orderly procedures, which gave us our "apple pie order" meaning today.

Armed to the Teeth

The first to be armed to the teeth was an ancient Nordic tribe known as the Berserkers, whose teeth were their most deadly weapons. These particular tribesmen were known for filing their teeth into sharp points and savagely attacking their opponents, who most often carried more civilized weapons like swords, spears, or clubs. Originally, "armed to the teeth" meant to be barely armed at all, but historically, its meaning of "being on the attack, prepared for any confrontation" carries over today.

Assassin

Assassins were named for a secret sect of Muslims who, during the Crusades, terrorized the Christians with their cultlike murders. Members of the tribes committed the murders under the influence of hashish (or hash, as we know it today) given to them by their leaders. The Arabic word for hashish is *hashashin*. Thus, the original assassins took their name from the drug they ingested to commit the crime.

Backseat Driver

Think "backseat driver" and you think of one who complains, or one who thinks he can see better from the rear than from the front of a vehicle. But the original backseat drivers weren't complainers. Matter of fact, for what they were watching, they *could* see better! In the days of the early fire engines, there was a job for backseat drivers. Someone needed to watch the ladder as engines rushed to the scene. As quick turns and abrupt stops were cause for accidents, a backseat driver was as vital a part of the fire team as the firefighters themselves.

Baker's Dozen

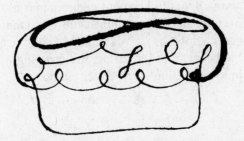

In the olden days, bakers who had shortchanged their customers by selling lighter loaves of bread were fined heavy penalties. So in 1266, English Parliament passed strict weight restriction laws that scared bakers into making sure they never came up short. Since weights could vary per loaf, it became customary for bakers to add a thirteenth loaf for good measure. So a baker's dozen came to mean thirteen.

Balk

To balk . . . to stop short, to pause before proceeding as though an obstacle were in the way is, by definition, a word to stop for. The word itself comes from the Old English *balca*, or beam. In the days before locks, these beams were placed across doors to keep out enemies and intruders. Because the beam stopped those attempting to enter a door, as well as stalled the one removing the beam from the inside, the meaning of stopping or stalling carries over today.

Ballpark Number

In the late 1800s, with the increasing popularity of baseball, ballparks became the hangout for large events, both sports-related and otherwise. Political candidates often found ballparks the best setting for their rallies, but because no tickets were sold for these events, newspaper reporters were forced to estimate a ballpark number in covering the attendance. When one party would overestimate its attendance for the press, the rival party would in turn do the same, and as a result, ballpark figures turned out to be very rough, often inaccurate counts.

Beating Around the Bush

No need beating around the bush, unless you're a hunter looking for game. As many hunters will tell you, it is sometimes necessary to scare the game into running or flying before one can shoot. Beating the bushes was a customary hunting procedure long ago. Yet, for one who really did not enjoy the sport of killing an animal, beating around the bush was also a way to scare off game so that nothing was left for the confrontation.

Bedlam

In referring to a madhouse, Bedlam can be taken quite literally, as there was one named just that in London in the mid–thirteenth century. Originally the site was a priory called St. Mary's of Bethlehem. Later, the name was shortened to Beth'lem, and then later, Bedlam. Some three hundred years later, the site was turned into a house of detention for the mentally insane.

Being Beside Oneself

There was once an ancient spiritual belief that said man's body and soul could part if he was placed under great physical or emotional stress. Under such conditions, it was believed that the soul merely jumped out of the body, placing itself beside the body until the turmoil had subsided. (Sneezing is believed to have been one such stressful occasion, and to this day we say "God bless you" to keep the body clean until the spirit has time to reenter.)

Beyond the Pale

Pale we take from the Latin word *palus*, which was a stake or boundary marker that fenced the territory under rule by a certain nation. Paling, or pickets, were quite common as boundary markers in Roman times. Those believed to be beyond the bounds of social or moral decency were once literally exiled beyond the pale, or beyond the confines of civilization as determined by the townspeople.

Blackball

Early social clubs in England had a practice of voting for their initiates by dropping white balls or marbles into a ballot box. Those voting against a particular candidate dropped a black ball, hence the term. While the term was first coined in the late 1700s, the custom dates back to ancient Greek and Roman times. Even our word *ballot* today refers to voting by little balls.

Blackmail

If there is such a thing as blackmail, is there such a thing as whitemail? The answer is yes! Scottish farmers in the mid-sixteenth century paid their landlords by either silver (known as whitemail) or produce (blackmail). The latter was the least preferred, so it was often abused. When greedy landlords forced cashless tenants to pay far more in goods than they would have paid in silver, blackmail took on its negative connotation.

Blimp

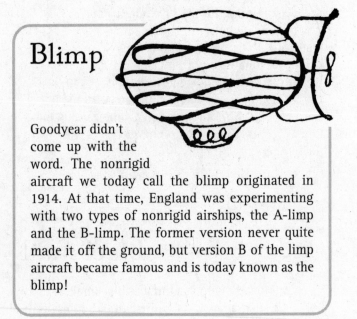

Goodyear didn't come up with the word. The nonrigid aircraft we today call the blimp originated in 1914. At that time, England was experimenting with two types of nonrigid airships, the A-limp and the B-limp. The former version never quite made it off the ground, but version B of the limp aircraft became famous and is today known as the blimp!

Boycott

The term *boycott* derives its name and its meaning from the first victim of its practice. In 1880, an absentee Irish landlord by the name of Lord Erne employed a Captain Charles Boycott to manage his estates. When Boycott pressed his tenants for unreasonably high rents, they refused to pay. In protest, the Irish Land League adopted the phrase to commemorate the action, and boycotting today gets its meaning from the event.

Bringing Home the Bacon

There is an old English custom whereby married couples who were willing to swear upon a Bible that they hadn't fought in a year were rewarded a side of bacon for their feat. Yet whether that custom gave us our current meaning for bringing home the bacon is doubtful. Most will tell you that "bringing home the bacon" is American in origin, and that it dates back to the greased pig contests of old county fairs. As the catcher was the keeper, the expression speaks for itself.

Bulls and Bears

The symbols we use today to refer to the status of the stock market actually began with the London stock market long ago. There, trading notices were posted (literally) on cork bulletin boards by hand. The British brokers of the eighteenth century called these stock bulletins "bulls," and you could find these bulls plastered on the board at the end of a heavy trading day. Obviously, when trading was less than busy, the bulletin board was bare, and the contrast of the two is how we came to call them bulls and bears today!

Cahoots

Cahoots were, quite simply, little cabins, or *kajuetes,* as they were called in medieval Germany. Often known to be occupied by bandits and robbers, these little cabins became the planning centers for attacks. So in reality, it was the goings-on *inside* the cabins that became known for what the cabins themselves were called. Today we use *cahoots* to refer to any shady partnership or less-than-upright scheme.

Calendar

The word *calendar* we take from the Latin word *calendarium,* which was a small book for keeping up with interest on loans. Interest, at the time, was due on the first day of every month (*calends* in Latin). The Latin verb for "to call" was *calere;* calendar was the combination of calling out that interest payments were due on the first day of the month!

Carte Blanche

Ask for carte blanche in France and you just might receive a white sheet of paper, because translated literally, that's what the term means. Custom has it that a man of importance would trust his closest subordinates with blank sheets or correspondence cards with only his name at the bottom, in order that they might use them for whatever needs they might have in a time of crisis. (Not much different from a blank check today.)

Catgut

When is a catgut not a catgut? When it's a sheep gut, which is what those nylonlike strings on guitars and tennis racquets are truly made of. So why the reference to cats, you ask? Because long ago, it was the substance used for stringing a kit (a small three-stringed violin, which was the forefather of today's guitar). The gut strings of the instrument might technically be called "kitguts," but a cat was never involved.

Charley Horse

Believe it or not, Charley was an actual horse! And when he got old, his owner decided to loan him to the keeper of the White Sox ballpark in Chicago in 1890, to pull the roller that laid the chalk lines for the baseball games there. Because old Charley was not in the prime of his life, he limped; and before long the crowd began to refer to any limping player on the team as "Old Charley Horse."

Chewing the Fat

Like so many colorful expressions, "chewing the fat" originated on the high seas. Think back to the early days of sailing, *pre*-refrigeration, when the only foods carried on long trips were those requiring no refrigeration. One such item was salt pork. As no part of the meat went to waste (including the skin), chewing the fat was common fare between meals (sometimes the fat was eaten as the meal itself!). It was in the late 1870s that "chewing the fat" became the catch-phrase for idle chatter that originally went along with the *real* chewing that took place aboard ships of old.

Clean as a Whistle

You might not think of a whistle as being so clean that we'd use it as a measure, but if you ever tried to make one from a reed (as they were made originally), then you'd understand the phrase. To obtain the pure wind sound derived from a reed whistle, the tube must be totally free of debris—clean and dry! So to have a thing clean as a whistle today means to have it as orderly as possible, with nothing blocking the passageways.

Cold Shoulder

The first cold shoulder referred to a cold shoulder of meat, given to a sojourner who might stop along the course of his travels to ask for food. As mutton was a common dish of old English farmhouses, it was customary for a traveler to be given a cold shoulder and be sent along his way. A warm meal would have indicated an invitation to stick around a bit longer; a cold shoulder was a sign that the traveler would be fed, but should expect no more.

Cooking One's Goose

One story has it that it was Eric, king of Sweden, in the mid-1500s, who hit upon a certain village with a handful of his best soldiers to overtake the land. As the townspeople watched, they soon determined that Eric's soldiers were neither numerous nor skilled, so the threat of the siege soon diminished. In mockery, the locals hung a goose in the middle of town for target practice for the king's men. As the story goes, King Eric became so angry that he burned the entire village, cooking goose and all! The phrase was popularized by a London ballad some years later.

Crocodile Tears

Those insincere tears we've come to know as crocodile tears are quite literal in origin. For you see, a crocodile does indeed cry over its meal as it eats. But the crying has nothing to do with the croc's sense of the situation. Instead, as a crocodile eats, his food is pressed to the top of his mouth, causing pressure against the glands known as the lachrimals. These secrete a tearlike substance that flows from the eyes. From this biological activity of the reptile, we today draw our meaning for crocodile tears.

Dandelions

No, this cute little flower didn't get its name from looking like an actual lion! Matter of fact, the *dande* part has nothing to do with our word *dandy* at all. Rather, it all goes back to the French, who called this fuzzy little flower *dent de lion, not* for the flower but for the leaves, thought to look like jagged lion's teeth. *Dent* (base word for our dental terminology) *de* ("of the") *lion* literally translates into "tooth of the lion."

Dark Horse

A couple of stories claim this expression, and they both have to do with the early days of horse racing. Some horse enthusiasts felt that dyeing the coat of their horse to a darker shade gave them better odds (even if the horse had a poor track record). Another story says a light horse could be raced twice if the color was changed to dark. Either way, the horse was a long shot of a bet. And if you're wondering why they never tried the same trick in reverse, like taking a bunch of brunette horses and making them blondes, well, they said it couldn't be done. (Obviously, at least where horses are concerned, blondes really *don't* have more fun!)

Dead as a Doornail

What *is* a doornail, anyway? Well, I'm here to tell you. The doornail is that plate or knob upon which a door's knocker knocks! As it *never* moves, and is pounded upon repeatedly, we assume it's dead. Hence the reference. (Some things are just too simple!)

Deadbeat

The first deadbeats were technically "debt beaters." These were people who avoided their creditors by leaving their debts behind. In the early days of this country, there were two ways to shirk your financial obligations: (1) by declaring bankruptcy, or (2) by actually moving out of the colony where the debt was incurred. Those choosing the latter were known as debt beaters, which later was shortened and mispronounced as deadbeats.

Dessert

It was the French who gave us both the word and the custom of dessert. By definition, their word *desservir* means "to clear the table," which originally consisted of clearing both dishes and tablecloth to make way for the final presentation. Most often that final course was a pastry or ice cream, but in all cases it was something sweet to end the meal. It was believed then that the sugar in the dessert was necessary to give a rush of energy in order that all the foods consumed during the meal could be digested.

Devil's Advocate

The role of the original DA was a religious one. (Who'd have thought it!) It all started with the Roman Catholic Church. When a name was submitted for canonization, two advocates were appointed to debate the matter to the fullest extent. One played the role of God's advocate. The other—the devil's. Together, the two brought up every possible argument in a case before a final decision was made.

Dingbat

Yes, there truly was an original dingbat! And it wasn't Edith Bunker. Rather, its origins date to vaudeville, where sticks were often used for sound effects from the stage (see *Slapstick*). Bells were also used at the punch line of a joke. This same stick was used for both batting the bells that marked the comic's buffoonery, and for sounding the final curtain call. From this association, *dingbat* soon became the word to comically describe one whose mental capacity was in question.

Dog Days

Oh, to get through those hot, hot days of summer . . . (Those dog-gone dog days!) Coined by the Romans as *caniculares dies* (days of the dog star), these are the seven hottest days of summer that fall (in our hemisphere) under the constellation Canis Major, in which Sirius is the brightest star. Sirius (also known as the Dog Star) was named for the Egyptian god whose head resembled that of a dog. So brilliant was this star that the Romans believed its rising contributed to the heat of the summer.

Dressed to the Nines

No, this doesn't mean that on a scale from one to ten one is dressed almost perfectly. The expression is English in origin, and was (when spoken correctly) "dressed to thy'n eyes" (quite obviously in reference to one spiffed up from head to toe). Leave it to us to make it slang, mispronounce it a bit, and make it a popular expression, even though "dressed to the nines," in and of itself, makes absolutely no sense!

Drumming Up Trade

Once in town, the early traveling sales-man had to play the role of PR man, advertising man, and musician all in one. In order to stir up business, he was often known to beat a drum or ring a bell. The former action gave us our catchphrase, "drumming up trade," while the latter lent itself to "Now, *that* rings a bell!"

Drunk as a Fiddler

To appreciate the meaning of this one, you have to go back to the origins of fiddle playing as a profession. The earliest paying gigs were most often for local weddings and wakes, and since most commoners couldn't afford a musician, it was customary for the fiddlers to play for food and drink. Many earned the reputation of taking full advantage of this trade, and soon the phrase "drunk as a fiddler!" was born.

Dyed in the Wool

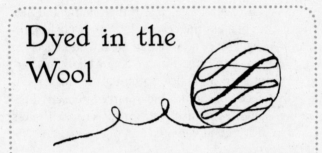

Those who work with wool know that if you attempt to dye an item after it is already spun into cloth, the odds of having an even, colorfast result are slim to none. The proper way to dye wool is to color the raw material before it is ever woven. By the same token, one said to be "dyed in the wool" is a person who is thoroughly indoctrinated with a belief, who believes in his cause through and through, and who leaves no gaps, no holes, no openings for any change in his opinion.

Earmark

Long ago in England, farmers found it helpful to mark the ears of their cattle and pigs to prevent thievery. Matter of fact, earmarking worked so well that the law soon decided that one caught in the act of taking an earmarked animal, or altering one to make it his own, should be earmarked himself (literally!) as punishment for the crime. (I guess if it's good enough for a pig . . . ?)

Ear to the Ground

It was the early American Indian who was first credited with keeping an ear to the ground. Perhaps you were told (as the first frontiersmen believed) that this was done in order to listen for horses' hooves as cowboys approached. However, Native American Indians will tell you the custom had to do with a certain spiritual belief. As they felt the land was sacred, most Indians held the view that listening to Mother Earth would protect them. To do this, they placed their ears to the ground in order to hear her heartbeat, and to be one with her nature.

Eat Crow

As the War of 1812 was coming to a close, story has it that an American soldier crossed British lines while hunting for game. Finding nothing better, the American shot a crow, but being overheard by a British officer, the soldier was forced to eat the crow as punishment for being on British soil. As the story goes, halfway through the act, the American turned on the British soldier, making *him* eat the remaining crow. As a result, eating crow came to mean having to do something that one simply did not want or mean to do.

Eavesdropping

Eavesdropping goes back to the old country, when property owners could not build their houses right up to their property lines. Instead, they had to leave space for the eaves, and the drippings from the rain and weather. The "eavesdrip" was that space between the houses, roughly two feet wide, wherein a nosy neighbor could easily drop by to overhear his neighbor's business.

Eccentric

Think of the most eccentric person you know, and I bet you're thinking "Strange!" By definition, the eccentric personality is one that falls "outside the normal pattern of behavior." But more specifically, the word *eccentric* is a geometric one. It is derived from the Greek word *ekkentros* (*ex* meaning "out of," *kentron* meaning "center"), and the precise translation is "off center," or just a little out of balance. Makes perfectly good sense that the eccentric personality is one that is just a little off the mark!

Egging One On

Candidly prompting or teasing one into something has nothing to do with eggs as we know them. Some will tell you the reference is to *ecgs*, which were the points of the spears the Norman invaders used. Our British cousins, however, say egging someone on is simply a mispronunciation of their more proper "edging on," and that we (once again) just slurred it over time.

Extremes

By definition, going to extremes means going way out of range, or going out of bounds. The original extremes were places in the early Middle Ages. From the Latin word *extremus*, the extremes were areas of land set just beyond the boundary of town, designated solely for the socially outcast. As this area was situated as far from the center of town as was possible, extremes became synonymous with living way out of bounds due to one's behavior being way out of line.

Face the Music

When you think of one who faces the music, perhaps you think of a symphony conductor or a band leader. Good guess, but obviously from the connotation of the phrase, the meaning is far less pleasant. Its origin is with the U.S. Army, and the music here refers to "Rogue's March," which was the tune played when an offender was cast out of the service, which was as disgraceful a moment as one could face.

Falsehood

In the Middle Ages, it was customary for men to wear cloaks with hoods indicating their professions. Doctors were known by one style of hood, clergymen another, artists and musicians yet another. In associating hood style with profession, most anyone could tell at a glance what business a man was in. Unfortunately, the downside to this concept came when someone attempted to pass himself off as a professional in a field for which he had no background. In such a case, the false hood worn gave meaning to the deception attempted.

Fiasco

By definition, a fiasco is a total, foolish failure, but for its origin, you'll have to go back to the glassblowers of Italy, who created beautiful bottles. The story has it that if a bottle was noted to have a flaw, it was set aside and reworked into a flask (*fiasco* in Italian). Not as artsy, but more practical in function was the re-created piece that was salvaged.

Fighting Fire with Fire

This one originated in America exactly as we coined it. Early settlers, in an effort to put out great prairie fires, learned that by setting ablaze a circle or a strip of land in the path of the fire, they could often lessen its impact. When the blaze hit barren land and there was nothing left for the fire to feed upon, it was more readily controlled. Soon the phrase became easily understood as "a dangerous measure to solve a dangerous problem."

Filling the Bill

"Filling the bill" came to us via early theatrical troupes. Around the early nineteenth century, acting groups began advertising by way of handbills. In order to fill up the page, it was common to print the name of the star in extra-large letters. When a star's performance lived up to the bold recognition of the handbill, he or she was said to have "filled the bill," thus living up to the hype.

Flash in the Pan

It was the early flintlock musket that required a pan for the priming powder to spark the flint. Often when one pulled the trigger of a musket, nothing happened, because the hammer that struck the flint did not generate a spark strong enough to ignite the powder. To watch the spark fizzle in the shallow pan holding the powder gave us our image of a flash in the pan. To this day we hold its meaning to be something that dazzles, but doesn't get the job done.

Fly-by-Night

We think of fly-by-nights as those shady, less-than-honorable businesses or businesspeople that are here one day, then gone the next. But the first reference to a fly-by-night was a superstitious one that described, quite literally, a witch! Because she flew by broom at night, the witch was seen as evil in nature, and up to no good. (In England, however, the fly-by-night had a totally different origin, so be careful if you use this phrase in Europe! There, fly-by-nights were once prostitutes, who did their business in the darkness of night, and flew away by the light of day.)

Fly off the Handle

The first thing to lose its head and fly off the handle was the common ax, and it was the early pioneers who gave us this phrase. Axes were made by hand, with the blade hammered out by blacksmiths or steelworkers. Handles were whittled by frontiersmen, and as a result, the fit wasn't always the best. At times, it was common to see an ax head fly right off the handle, mid-chop, often hurting nearby woodsmen. This unexpected trouble soon became synonymous with anger and the loss of control. The image, as a figure of speech, just stayed with us through time.

Freelance

A self-employed writer, photographer, or whatever, is not the same as those who first called themselves freelancers. The earliest were medieval Italian and French knights, known as "free companions," who would sell their lancing skills to any master. The freelance title was said to be first used by Sir Walter Scott in his novel *Ivanhoe*.

Freeloader

The first sponging off of others, or free-loading, as the word is used, took place in the pubs of merry old England. Unofficial rules once had it that when five or six friends got together to drink, each would pay for a round, until all had contributed to the evening. One who would accept drinks and then leave the pub before his turn to pay basically got loaded for free, hence the term *freeloader*. (Interesting to note that in northern England, the one who left early was said to be "shy his pint of beer," and was thus called a pint-shyer, as opposed to a freeloader.)

Garden

A word we take for granted, but one with an interesting origin all the same, the *gardin,* as it was originally spelled in Old English, was a most sacred place. Because they contained the substance of life, gardens, in medieval times, were the responsibility of monks; as a result, you could find one near every abbey and monastery. Before long, the monks devised walls and fences to protect these sacred plots, areas referred to as the "guarded" lands. Later translated, *garden* soon came to stand for any land set aside for growing, guarded with walls or not.

Gerrymandering

Every history buff should know this one. The date: 1812. The place: Essex County, Massachusetts. Governor Elbridge Gerry, a Democrat, wanted to increase his party's power in the state senate, so he worked out a redistricting plan that they swear looked just like a salamander! Benjamin Russell, editor of the *Columbian Sentinel,* is believed to have coined the phrase.

Getting One's Goat

It was common practice in the early days of horse racing to place a goat in the stall with a high-strung pacer to calm him before the race. The two made good roommates, but before long, it also became common practice for an opponent to steal his competitor's goat, in order to upset his horse before the race. Many a good racehorse was ruined by someone getting his goat!

Goblin

While several accounts exist for the origin of *goblin,* perhaps the most popular dates back to the early 1400s. At that time a beautiful bright red fabric came out of Paris, created by Gilles and Jehan Gobelin. So stunning was this cloth that Louis XIV declared their factory a royal business. With this, the superstitious and jealous locals of the day started rumors suggesting that the brothers must have sold their souls to the devil in exchange for the sudden good fortune. As a result, the *Gobelins* were ostracized, and their names were made synonymous with the word we now associate with evil or mischief.

God Bless You

Ever wonder why we would have "God bless you" after a sneeze? Well, in much the same way that it was believed man could part body and spirit and be beside himself, the ancients believed a good sneeze could literally blast your soul right out of your body! To ensure that no bad spirits moved into the vacancy, "God bless you" was said to clear the way so soul and body could reunite.

Going to the Dogs

Hard to imagine, but dogs of olden days and often of other countries didn't live the high life they do today. Historically, living a dog's life meant groveling for food, sleeping on the ground, and fighting for territory. Dog food, as we know it, would've been laughable then, as only the garbage considered worthless to humans went to the dogs.

Gone to Pot

Some more morbid souls might tell you that this phrase refers to one's ashes following a cremation. But in reality, the phrase goes back to Elizabethan times and the original beef stew, when leftover meat scraps, too small for anything other than stew bites, were thrown into the big pot over the stove and boiled for hours. When good for nothing else, scraps always went to pot!

Goose Pimples

Also known as gooseflesh, goose pimples are those bumps you get when your skin takes a chill. For obvious reasons, goose pimples were named for their similarity to the skin of a plucked goose. Long ago, goose feathers were used for a myriad of things; thus, some birds were plucked up to five times a year. From these pluckings, farmers soon noticed the reaction of gooseflesh to the cold, as the birds' skin contracted to pull up what would have been feathers. This gooseflesh was soon associated with the same bumpy-skin effect that cold or certain emotions had on humans.

(Up for) Grabs

This one we borrowed from the Great Depression, when diners and cafeterias found it customary to save every scrap of food. Any and all excess was salvaged, and restaurant owners soon started setting aside their leftovers for beggars and the homeless. It became the practice for these leftover scraps to be set at the end of the lunch counter, bagged and ready to go, for anyone who might be in need. Thus, the expression "up for grabs" became the catchphrase for those morsels of food, set *up* on the counter for the needy to *grab*.

Great Scott!

If you don't know which Scott we're referring to here, you should, so take note! Great Scott refers to one Winfield Scott, commander of the Mexican War and the Whig party's nomination for president in the election of 1852. Scott was known for being rather stuck on himself, and his campaign was marked with pride and arrogance, yet he campaigned with great fervency. His opposition referred to him as "Great Scott!" making fun of his pomposity, and as a result, we use the phrase pretentiously today. (Incidentally, Great Scott was defeated by Franklin Pierce. It just goes to show . . .)

Guinea Pig

While the guinea pig has long been associated with laboratory experimentation, the connotation of a used person is much more colorful. Early stock companies in England often acquired noblemen to sign on as their directors for the sake of credibility. The only legal obligation was that the figurehead attend an annual meeting (usually a luncheon or dinner), where he was paid a director's fee of one guinea (approximately twenty-one shillings). The pun referred to the token fee, and the free meal typically received for allowing the company to use his name.

Ham

Ever wonder about the theatrical term *ham*? Well, it's short for ham fatter, which goes way back to the early days of acting and the blackface comedians. The practice of greasing the face with ham fat in order to remove makeup separated the blackface actors from the more seriously theatrical (and less made-up) white faces.

Happy as a Clam

Tell me you haven't wondered about this one! Who says clams are happy, anyway? Did the government do a clam study? Well, to explain it, we must first look at the phrase in its entirety, which is "happy as a clam at high tide." Since clams are usually plucked up at low tide, the phrase simply means they've been left alone. (A stretch, yes, but it's all ours! First recorded in 1834.)

Hat in the Ring

There *was* an actual ring that gave us the image of politicians tossing their hats in the ring in announcing their desire to run for public office. That ring was in Vienna, Austria, still known today as "the Ringstrasse," or Ring Street. Those seeking public office were known to frequent this famous center, not only to address the crowds about their candidacy, but to solicit support (hat in hand) for campaign contributions. The concept and phrase are said to have made it to America by way of our Austrian immigrants.

Haul over the Coals

While we use this expression to connote a thorough questioning, the original hauling was far more grueling, as it was quite literal. Dating back to England in the Middle Ages, a haul over the coals was the test for someone accused of heresy in the Old Country. The accused would be forced to walk barefoot over a bed of glowing embers. If the suspect survived, he or she was acquitted, believed to be truly of God. If, however, the suspect flinched, stumbled, or worse, the verdict was "guilty as charged" and the hauling ended in death. Most confessed to avoid the walk altogether.

Having a Screw Loose

It's easy enough to conjure up the image of a machine with a screw loose, but which machine originally gave us the phrase? Well, it was the cotton gin, the advent of which caused cotton mills to multiply at an unbelievable rate in the late 1700s. So frequent were the breakdowns of the earliest machines that loose screws were nearly always blamed for the problem. As a result, the phrase was adapted by most everyone who needed to blame something or someone for just about anything. By the early 1800s, having a screw loose became the catchphrase for something gone amiss.

Heebie-Jeebies

Cartoonist Billy DeBeck is credited with coining this phrase in the late 1940s, but the origin traces back even further. It is believed that DeBeck took the name from a dance made popular in the early 1900s. One story has it that the name derives from a Native American source describing the gestures made by Indian witch doctors before a sacrifice. Yet other sources credit the words *hiba jiba*, as first noted by European missionaries visiting the African Congo. *Hiba jiba* was literally translated as one "out of his skin," and it was the reaction believed to be caused by evil spirits leaving the body. The *hiba jiba* of old became the "heebie jeebies" we know as a dance move. That same agitated, jittery feeling is credited for the expression we refer to as heebie-jeebies today.

Heyday

Heydays of old were literally feast days, and were a product of the feudal system. In medieval times, a serf who tended to his lord's manor was entitled to both military protection and a portion of the harvest. In addition to the produce that a serf might take for his family, he was given one hay day each year to store up hay for his livestock. This "payment day" was usually set aside at the end of each harvest (somewhere in mid-October) and was followed by great celebration and feasting, which gives the word its association today.

Hick

The country hick is quite American in origin, dating back to the early American schoolrooms. As the need for formal education increased, so did theories on how best to instruct. Controversial were the precepts of corporal punishment, and many of the more progressive thinkers challenged its value. Those country folk who held to the belief of "spare the rod and spoil the child" were said to be from "hickory towns," those towns whose schools still utilized hickory sticks in disciplining their schoolchildren. From that, we condensed and created our word *hick* today.

High on the Hog

Okay: Pig Anatomy 101. Things high on the hog include: tenderloin, bacon, pork chops, spare ribs, and ham (i.e., basically the better parts we've grown to know and love, especially here in the South!). Incidentally, low-on-the-hog parts include pigs' feet, knuckles, and jowls. Not a hard one to understand, especially in light of food allocations on Southern plantations. The big house ate high. The slaves ate low. The expression speaks for itself!

High Seas

Ahoy, matey! What's this talk of high seas? Well, by definition, the high seas are specifically those seas that are purely public—the property of *no* country. (Rules have it that a country can only lay claim to water three miles from its borders.) High seas are public domain, just as highways are for public use *within* a country.

Hobnob

Taken from the Old English, *hobnob* literally translates "have and have not," or "to give and take." In taverns of old, that's exactly what transpired. Famous for socializing in their local pubs, the English were quick to offer a toast on behalf of their closest friends. As one had to give and another receive, hobnobbing was quite the social event of the day. And as drinks were bought in rounds (see *Freeloader*), the word *hobnob* had as much to do with the giving and taking of information as it did with the giving and taking of ale!

Hooker

The slang for prostitute is almost as old as the profession, and there is more than one possibility for its origin. One theory suggests prostitutes working the British ports at the Hook of Holland coined the phrase. The American version says that General Joseph Hooker gave us the term during Civil War days when he forbade his men to hang out in the red-light district in Washington, D.C. Either way, the expression dates back to the world's oldest profession.

Hue and Cry

The public outcry we now refer to as hue and cry was, in its early day, a law enforcement tactic. Long ago, when one was robbed, he was said to yell "with hue and with cry" or "with horn and with voice." At this, the townspeople were to drop what they were doing and go in search of the criminal. The word *hue* we took from the French *huer,* which means "to shout." Add a "cry" to whatever evil befell you, and the alarm was triggered for the public to go after the offender. Today the phrase is synonymous with *any* loud disturbance, independent of criminal offense.

Idiot

The ancient Greeks were quick to distinguish between their public officials and their private citizens. The latter they called *idios,* which originally meant "private," but later came to mean "anyone mentally incapable of taking part in community affairs." (Funny how today we've come to value our private citizens, and are more and more finding our elected ones to be in the *idios* category!)

In a Jam

Believe it or not, "in a jam" has a history in the hunting arena, and the phrase is said to date back to the early 1800s. Appalachian frontiersmen were said to have discovered that homemade jam and fruit preserves were quite an attraction for animals such as raccoons, skunks, and even bears. Before long, jam became the bait for trappings. When a scavenger, lured by the smell of the fruits and seasonings, was caught in a jam, nearby hunters would shoot away. The phrase quickly spread throughout the East to describe any sticky or difficult situation.

In a Pretty Pickle

The phrase "in a pickle" came to us from the Dutch, and refers to the salt solution used some four centuries ago in preserving pickles. Yet, as pickle barrels were transported to this country, their juice was soon discovered to have other preserving qualities as well. Stored in barrels, in the hulls of large boats, this same pickled water was also found to be quite useful in preserving the occasional human who happened to die while making the trip across the seas. For one to be in a pickle meant he was in a poor state, indeed!

Indian Giver

History tells us that early American settlers had trouble comprehending the customs of the Native American Indians, who were known to take back a gift when another of equal value was not given in exchange. While the Native American Indians saw equality and fairness in the custom, the settlers saw it as inconsistent, and felt Indian giving was not a matter of giving at all.

Influenza

The common flu has a superstitious origin. The phrase was coined in the mid-1700s when the first outbreak of the virus was recorded in Rome. It was believed at the time that the stars *influenced* such evil and contagious epidemics, and *influenza* (the Italian word for influence) became the given name for this particular one!

In the Bag

The oldest reference to "in the bag" is said to have come from hunting lingo, with the "bag" being that used to bag game. But a more local and colorful explanation also exists. It has to do with cockfighting, the illegal competition between gamecocks (traditionally fitted with spurs) that fight until the death of one of the contestants. As prize gamecocks were usually transported in cloth bags, "cocky" owners have been credited with the phrase, as they boasted that their victory was in the bag prior to a fight ever taking place.

In the Doghouse

Not the doghouse you might recognize as Fido's, *this* doghouse originated with the first slaves brought to America. On the decks of the slave ships were small cubicles, referred to as doghouses because of their size and unappealing nature. Sailors in charge of watching the slaves were on doghouse duty, while the remaining crew stayed under locked hatches for safety's sake.

In the Groove

"In the groove" is actually one of our more recent expressions, and we're happy to claim it as purely American in origin. A product of the Swing Era, "in the groove" has to do with the advent of the phonograph, more specifically, the needle and the record. If you were into counting grooves, you would find that there is but one long, continuous groove per record. But only in keeping the phonograph needle in the groove can you be assured of keeping the music flowing smoothly.

In the Hole

To be in the hole, as it refers to being in debt, originated in the gambling houses of old. Poker was the preferred game of the mid-1800s, and it was during poker's popularity that gambling-house owners prospered. As a certain percentage of each game went to the house, cash was stuffed in a slot or hole in the center of each table. The money was secured in a box underneath. Those losers who wound up with more money in the hole than in their pockets were said to be in the hole. The association of being without cash has remained ever since.

In Two Shakes of a Lamb's Tail

Granted, a lamb *is* known to shake its tail twice as fast as most any other animal, but the expression seems to be an extension of a more popular British phrase, "in two shakes." Both refer to something done instantaneously, yet one was coined in the mid-1800s and refers to a small sheep, while the other dates back much later and has to do with the quick shaking of a dice box just before those dice are rolled.

Iron Curtain

While we most often credit Winston Churchill with this one, it is believed by historians to have actually been coined by Queen Elizabeth of Belgium in 1914. While the phrase refers to the strength and secrecy behind what once was the Soviet Union (and other Communist countries), it is believed the inspiration was derived from actual fireproof iron curtains used in European theaters long ago.

Jailbird

Historically speaking, punishment for crime has come in a variety of forms, but until most recently, one shared by most societies was public display. From the stockades to the guillotines, public punishments were events for all to see, serving as both deterrent and social gathering. At one time, it was common practice to imprison thieves and robbers in large iron cages, hung slightly above ground level for all to see. It was from this particular punishment that the word *jailbird* was coined, playing off the obvious resemblance of the criminal to a bird in a cage.

Jalopy

With the boom of the automobile industry, there soon was a glut of used cars, transported to Mexico, where production did not exist. In Jalapa, the capital city of Veracruz (also known for its jalapeño peppers), secondhand cars were restored and sold on the Mexican market. Before long, these cars became known as "Jalapa's cars" (pronounced with an *h* in Mexico), but today we just call the junkers "jalopies"!

Jaywalker

Early American settlers were unfamiliar with blue jays, which were plentiful in the New World. As our country expanded, these birds retreated farther into the countryside to avoid the big cities. Before long they became synonymous with mountain people and country hicks. Ignorant of traffic laws and other city customs, country folk who visited town soon became known as jaywalkers, or country birds in the city.

Jeep

As you probably know, these rugged, all-terrain vehicles were originally built for the U.S. Army, and were especially useful in times of war. When the first quarter-ton reconnaissance cars were delivered, the letters *G.P.* were painted on their doors, short for "General Purpose," which was precisely the function of these sturdy land-climbing jewels! The word *jeep* was simply a shorter, more familiar version of *G.P.*, as it was read on the doors of the vehicles.

Josh

Several stories exist for the word *josh*. One has it that the Scottish word *joss*, meaning to push against or jostle, may have started it all. Another theory has it that the word is early American and is a combination of *joke* and *bosh* (the latter meaning "foolish talk"). But whatever its origin, the popularity of *josh* came about when American humorist and writer Josh Billings—known for his misspelled words, humorous grammar, and literary puns—made it famous in the mid-1800s. Josh's name became synonymous with the joking style in which he wrote.

Jumbo

A fairly recent addition to our language, the word *jumbo* was first mentioned in reference to an elephant, purchased by P. T. Barnum in 1881. Jumbo was captured in West Africa in 1869 and was the largest elephant known to man at the time. Weighing in at six and a half tons, Jumbo was a favorite at the London Zoological Society, which is where P.T. found him. Barnum was reported to have paid $30,000 for Jumbo, and was said to have recouped his investment tenfold within six weeks. Thanks to Jumbo's size and P.T.'s marketing, *jumbo* became *the* word for the largest thing going!

Jump the Gun

While some hunters may tell you "jumping the gun" refers to game that takes flight prior to the shoot, the original meaning goes back to racing, specifically sprinting. Often a runner, so eager to run, jumps ahead of the starting shot, and that jump gives us our reference today.

Keeping Up with the Joneses

May we never forget! "Keeping Up with the Joneses" was a comic strip, made popular in the early 1900s. The creation of cartoonist Arthur ("Pop") Momand, it ran in American newspapers for more than twenty-eight years. Having struggled himself to keep up with others in classes above his own, Momand was said to have created the cartoon from his own experience before moving out of an upscale neighborhood with his wife. Interestingly enough, Momand originally considered "Keeping Up with the Smiths" as the name for his cartoon, but settled on Joneses, thinking it sounded better.

Kick the Bucket

This has nothing to do with kicking a pail out from under a man being hanged. The phrase originates in the slaughterhouses of old, where hogs were slashed and hung (by their heels) and strung by a pulley weighted with a wooden block called a bucket. (The name we borrowed from the bucket-in-the-well concept.) Often, in its last efforts at life, the slaughtered hog was known to kick the bucket, just before it gave up the ghost.

Kid Gloves

Short for "kidding gloves," kid gloves were first designed for the very wealthy in fourteenth-century England. Because workers of the day needed gloves to protect their hands, they found the fingerless, impractical gloves to be a joke, and thus referred to them as fake or kidding gloves. The phrase "to treat someone with kid gloves" was a further mockery of the upper class, as by all means they would never have need for gloves other than to show their social status. As a result, we today use the phrase to connote treating someone pretentiously special.

Kindergarten

Much like the word sounds, *kindergarten* was a term meaning "children's garden." It was coined by the nineteenth-century German instructor Friedrich Froebel, who believed that the mind of the child should be given the respect and attention one would give a garden. It was Froebel who came up with the concept of a school for the very young, to allow children the opportunity to play, to construct, and to exercise their minds, cultivating natural abilities and aptitudes in the confines of a schoolroom setting.

Kit and Caboodle

From the Dutch, the word *boedal* means "effects," or those things that a person owns. Thieves adapted the word, calling whatever they stole the "boodle." Pirates used the same reference in referring to the "booty" they took from ships they attacked. As burglars' tools were carried in their "kits," a clean sweep of a house was often referred to as getting away with "the kit and the boodle." It is from this combination that our phrase "kit and caboodle" was coined.

Kittycorner

Whether you call it kittycorner or whether you call it cattycorner, the term has nothing to do with felines. Instead, we take our "corner" from the French word *quatre* (meaning four). The true word is *catercorner*, with "cater" being defined as the point diagonally across a square.

Knock on Wood

So why would knocking on wood be a symbol for luck? It goes way back to pre-Christian times, when pagan religious beliefs held that good spirits resided in trees. To knock on a tree was to call upon those spirits to protect you as you journeyed through life (and especially through the forest!).

Knowing (Him/Her) Like a Book

To know a person inside and out, or to know him "like a book," goes back to the days when there were very *few* books. Matter of fact, the Bible would be one good example of just how the phrase came into being. Before printing presses made household items out of Bibles (and later, other books), people had to memorize scriptures and stories in order to pass the information along. Monks of old were perhaps the first to know something from cover to cover, as one would know a book, thus, the expression "speaks for itself."

Knowing the Ropes

Some will say these ropes are those that pulled the curtains in the early days of theater, but the phrase goes back to the beginning of the Royal Navy. From its inception, the task of turning vagabonds and other vagrants into seamen was a tough one. The complex network of rigs and ropes made for much to be learned, but to find one who knew the ropes (or to teach one) was an accomplishment indeed!

Knuckling Down

"Knuckling down" dates back to the game of marbles, which was quite popular as a children's sport in late-seventeenth-century England. As the rules required that each player shoot his or her marble from outside the drawn ring of play, "knuckling down" became *the* expression of the day, meaning "focused attention to any game at hand."

Lady

Perhaps *lady* today means a female of refined habits and gentle manners, but the original lady was hardly so stylish! From the Middle English word *ladie,* the first lady was nothing more than a "kneader of bread"! Before you jest, keep in mind that the lord of the manor was likewise named for being the "keeper of the bread." Together the two maintained their household. Seeing how lords and ladies were those who *had* households to maintain in the first place (as opposed to being mere workers for another), the first lady did hold some power through the food she produced.

Lame Duck

The original lame duck was a member of the British Stock Exchange who couldn't meet his liabilities on settlement date, and thus flew off without settling his account. From that we applied the term to our political candidates, who, by way of losing an election, can't return to the flock, even though their own party has been retained. Much as it would be for a wounded bird that could no longer fly, the lame duck candidate becomes the responsibility of the new administration, and is taken care of, often by being given some appointment to an office that requires no election.

Letting the Cat out of the Bag

Back in the Middle Ages, when the Muslims invaded Southern Europe, suddenly pork was declared unclean, and thus became a premium on the open market. Because of strict laws forbidding such, pigs were sold undercover, stashed in bags (or pokes, which some cite to credit the expression "pig in a poke"). On occasion, a cat was substituted for the more expensive pig, and it wasn't until the new owner let the cat out of the bag that the scam was revealed.

Lewd

From the Old English word *lǣwede*, this word was originally a label for the layperson, or one not in the clergy. As that most often meant one who was ignorant, the word was used to describe those who were unlearned, hence, common. From this, the definition was carried down to mean "base," and later took on the connotation of vulgar in both language and behavior. All from a simple attempt to separate the commoners from the more righteous clergy, the word *lewd* today now means sexually unchaste and all but evil.

Limelight

Originally, the limelight was a literal description and not just the catchphrase we know it as today. Early stage lighting (and earlier yet, lighthouse lighting) was made of calcium (or lime). Technically, a stream of oxygen crossed with hydrogen was burned on a lime surface, which gave out a brilliant white light. It was from early theatrical settings that we draw the spotlight meaning for one who stands in the limelight.

Lion's Share

The lion's share, meaning "all," or nearly all, comes from Aesop's fable about a lion, a fox, and an ass that went hunting. Upon returning with their kill, the lion asked the ass to divide their spoils, allotting each his share. The ass divided each share equally and allowed each partner to pick his own. At this, the lion roared and killed the ass, taking that part with his. The lion then asked the fox to divide the remaining goods, upon which the fox took only a small portion. When asked how he'd learned his math so well, the fox's reply was "By noting what happened to the ass!"

Lollypop

Some of our greatest words go back to the mother country, and *lollypop* is one such example. Even in some parts of England today, *lolly* is the word used for *tongue*. Take a piece of candy that pops in and out of your mouth (as is the case with our Americanized sucker) and you've got lollypop! (It just *sounds* more proper than our word, don't you think?)

Loophole

In castles of old, loopholes were a common architectural structure built into the walls themselves, as a form of security for times of war. These small openings, spaced every few feet apart, were designed both for observation as well as for firing small weapons like arrows. While the holes were small and narrow, if need be, they could serve as a rough means of escape should the castle be taken under attack. It is from this context that our current definition of a loophole, as a way out of a problem, came into being.

(At) Loose Ends

To find the original loose ends you've got to board a ship! When sailing vessels were first in vogue, knowing the ropes and finding the right rigs were key to successful travel. When work was slack, crew members were often made to repair those wind- and wave-damaged lines, braiding and tying off the loose ends. From this, a person "at loose ends" was one who was frayed, tattered, or weathered.

Lunatic

We get the word *lunatic* from the same base word that gives us *lunar,* which, of course, means it pertains to the moon. *Lunatic* was coined by the early Romans in reference to the mentally insane, as a description of one they thought was moonstruck. For centuries, man has believed that full moons have had an effect on behavior. The Romans simply gave it a name, and we still use it today!

Mad as a Hatter

In the early days of felt hats, mercury was used as a processing agent, and as a result, many hat makers of the day developed mental and neurological problems (it is now believed) from their handling of the poisonous substance. Soon, the saying "mad as a hatter" became synonymous with anyone suffering from a mental imbalance. Lewis Carroll later popularized the phrase with his Mad Hatter character in the story of Alice in Wonderland.

Mad as a March Hare

While Lewis Carroll may have popularized this expression to the degree we know it today, the origins of "mad as a March hare" go back as far as Chaucer. Some say the original expression was "mad as a marsh hare," claiming that hares near open marshes were more animated (if not visible) than those in covered hedges. The buck hare in particular has long been noted for its frolicking antics as it springs into its mating season. Thanks to those who have given their lives to observing such, the mad March hare is today synonymous with utter lunacy.

Make No Bones about It

In days of old, when cooking was done over an open fire, it wasn't uncommon to find a variety of items all cooking in one pot. Often, scraps of meat were tossed in the mix (see *Gone to Pot*), and as a result, bones were pretty much inevitable. True, it required a degree of caution as you ate, seeing as you might run across a bone in your stew. Yet while the more particular guest might complain of the bones in his bowl, those who simply appreciated the meal, making no big deal of the occasional inconvenience, were said to have made "no bones about it."

Making One's Mark

While many may hope to make their mark in the world, few perhaps actually do so. Nonetheless, at one point in time, making one's mark meant simply distinguishing one's work from another's. More specifically, it was the practice of smiths and artisans of long ago to mark their wares with a symbol or logo placed somewhere on the art piece. Once that mark became generally well known, the artist was said to have "made his mark" in the world, thus indicating true success.

Maudlin

The word we use today to mean weak, insipid, or emotional came to us from biblical times. The word *maudlin* was the British pronunciation of Magdalene—more specifically, Mary Magdalene of Jesus' day. As medieval painters depicted Mary Magdalene with doleful face and swollen eyes from her weeping over the death of her lord, *maudlin* soon became synonymous with sadness, melancholy, and depressive expressions, which we know it for today.

Maverick

It was in Texas around the mid-1800s that cattle branding was all the rage for ranches wanting to identify their cattle as their own. It was Samuel Maverick, owner of one of the largest ranches around, who decided that in *not* branding his cattle would they be best identified. Maverick declared that any cattle found without a brand were his own. As this method would've included all wild and unclaimed beasts as well his own, his attempts failed. Soon, his name became synonymous with anything that hadn't been claimed by a prior group.

Mind Your P's and Q's

Two explanations are offered for the origins of "p's and q's": One pertains to pubs, the other, to the early printing press. The former states that "p's and q's" date back to English taverns of the seventeenth century, when it was the responsibility of the bartender to keep up with the beer consumption of his patrons. Watching the pints and quarts of ale consumed prompted the friendly reminder, "Now, mind your p's and q's" (the historic prelude to "Don't drink and drive"). A second reference dates back to early printing presses, when typeset letters were placed by hand. As set type was a mirror opposite of its print on the page, it was easy to confuse p's with q's, thus generating the mindful adage to pay close attention to the tiniest of details.

Nag

That annoying, irritating word *nag* comes from the Scandinavian word *nagga,* which means "to gnaw." It was during the Middle Ages that rat infestation in Europe was fairly common. This, coupled with squirrels that often nested in thatched roofs, made for gnawing, annoying sounds throughout the night. It was from this nerve-racking sound that the shortened word *nag* was formed. By comparison, one who gnaws at another by way of complaining with that annoying sound of rat-gnawing, *nag* has taken on its current meaning today.

Name Is Mud

Legend has it that the mud referred to in this context has to do with Dr. Samuel Mudd, the hapless physician whose fame in life came from setting the broken leg of John Wilkes Booth shortly after the assassination of President Abraham Lincoln. Though strictly abiding by his profession's code of ethics, Dr. Mudd was, as a result of his action, sentenced to a life in prison for helping an assassin. (Point of interest: Even in prison, Mudd gained recognition for the tremendous contribution he made in working with patients of the typhoid epidemic.)

Nepotism

The word *nepotism,* used to describe favoritism to a relative within a professional context, was first coined during the reign of Pope Alexander VI (1492–1503). Noted as perhaps the most political pope of all, Alexander is remembered for filling more positions within the church by way of his own relatives than any other pope in history. Direct from the Latin word *nepos,* nepotism originally referred to any descendant, especially a nephew or grandson. Today the word includes any and all family shown favoritism strictly on the basis of kinship.

Nest Egg

The first nest eggs were made out of clay and placed in a hen's nest to inspire the laying of more eggs. (Today, farmers just leave one real egg for the same effect.) Soon the same notion was applied to humans, with the nest egg representing that stash of savings set aside in an effort to motivate a person to lay aside more!

Nickname

Another mispronunciation slurred over time . . . *nickname* was originally pronounced "ekename," with *eke* meaning "extra" in Old English. This ekename, or "extra name," made sense by definition, as many folks are called by one name though given another. Nonetheless, because we aren't too articulate, over time, *nickname* is the ekename that stuck!

Nick of Time

Tally sticks nicked to keep count at various sporting events were common some time ago. Nicking was invented when these games required a scorekeeping system fair to all. The same system became a practical tool in both early churches as well as in British Parliament for keeping up with attendance. The trick was to arrive before the count got to your seat, or to arrive in the nick of time!

Nightmare

The Old English word *mare* described a certain kind of evil spirit, imagined to be female, thought to be much like a goblin or monster. The nightmare was believed to disturb a person's sleep by sitting on the chest of the sleeper, causing a feeling of suffocation and terror in the night. As a result, the term *nightmare* later became the word for both the spirit as well as the feeling produced. Today we simply use it to describe any frightening dream or experience that occurs while one is sleeping.

Nincompoop

Some historians say our word *nincompoop* originated with the Latin phrase *"non compos mentis,"* which translates to "without ability" or "of unsound mind." Certainly that meaning holds true for *nincompoop,* as used today to imply a fool or a simpleton.

Nip It in the Bud

The gardeners among us will understand this one right away, as some plants will grow excessively if not controlled. Pruning is key here, and horticulturists have known for centuries that nipping the bud of the plant prevents it from producing fruit. It was in Shakespeare's day that this gardening phrase became synonymous with "instantly ending a project or plan before it grows out of control."

Nitwit

While this one is American in origin, *nitwit* is a combination of both English and German words. The *nit* we take from the German word *nicht*, meaning "no." Add that to our English word *wit* (intelligence) and you have one with "no wits" or with no sense at all! (Don't you love it when cultures cross-pollinate?)

Not Worth One's Salt

Anyone not worth his salt is worth very little indeed, and by some definitions, not worth the money he earns. In days of old, the Romans were known to give rations of salt and other necessities to their soldiers and civil servants. These portions fell under the general category of *sal* (in Latin), and when money became the substitute, the word *salarium* (base for our word *salary*) was born. In a reversed context, the English phrase "true to his salt" refers to one faithful to his employer.

Odds and Ends

The first official odds and ends were found in lumberyards, as they were, quite literally, leftover scraps of wood. Odds were those pieces of board split irregularly by the sawmill that were less than even in shape. The ends were those end pieces trimmed from boards that were cut to specific lengths. Some dishonest lumberers were said to have sold these odds and ends to unknowing customers by adding the inches of the pieces in question, and including them in the total footage count upon delivery.

Off Color

While many theories exist for the origin of this phrase, one of the more predominant ones has to do with the early days of night-clubs and the colored spotlights focused on the featured performer. As hosts and emcees were often known to work their material in between acts, some were known to use their less clean versions to the side of center stage, thereby dodging the spotlight if the audience took offense. From this "off-color performance" do some claim the phrase took on its risqué meaning today.

Off the Cuff

Working "off the cuff" goes back to the pubs of old England, where bartenders, dressed in starched white shirts, were often known to keep up with their customers' bar tabs by writing on the cuffs of their shirtsleeves. Come time to clear that tab, the quick bartender was able to give the total owed, right off the cuff!

O.K.

The initials O.K. refer to a certain political organization formed in support of presidential candidate Martin Van Buren, when he was running for reelection in 1840. The members supporting Van Buren formed "the Democratic O.K. Club," with the *O.K.* standing for Old Kinderhook, New York, a nickname given Van Buren that was taken from his hometown of Kinderhook, located in the Hudson Valley. As O.K. became the catchphrase of the day, its meaning soon came to be known as "all right," and it holds that same association today.

One Fell Swoop

So what's a swoop, and why did it fall? Well, first of all, it didn't. The *fell* in this context refers not to falling, but to "cruel" or "mean." (It is derived from the same root word as *felon*.) "One fell swoop," then, was coined to describe one mean or cruel bird of prey, swooping down to attack its victim. That same dive-bomb approach has since been borrowed to describe other similarly dramatic situations.

On the Carpet

When carpets were first introduced, only the well-to-do could afford to cover their floors. As this meant only the master or mistress of the house would have carpeted rooms, it was fair to say that the servants only stood on carpets when they were called in for a reprimand or termination. From this practice, dating back to the early 1800s, our current meaning for one called "on the carpet" came into being.

On the Nose

To "*win* by a nose" goes back to early horse racing days, but to "*be* on the nose" takes us back to the early days of radio. Since the first radio broadcasts were staged live in a studio, with the director across the way in a soundproof booth, hand signals were critical in timing the show's elements. The hand sign for cueing out on time was finger to nose, and we've since taken the phrase to mean anything perfectly timed.

On the Wagon

The original wagon on which reformed alcoholics pledged to stay was the horse-drawn water cart of the late 1800s. In the heyday of Prohibition, many a reformer would take a vow to stop drinking alcohol, substituting water as their liquid refreshment. A backslider was said to have fallen off the (water) wagon and back onto hard liquor or moonshine.

Ouija Board

Pronounced "wee-jee" board, the original tool for receiving communication from the spirit world was designed for simple yes-or-no questions. However, the name *Ouija* was formed from the French word *oui* and the German word *ja*, which actually makes the first Ouija board a "yes-yes" board!

Overwhelm

Interestingly enough, *overwhelm* means basically the same as *whelm,* though *over* adds more emphasis. It's the *whelm* part that adds its meaning. From the Middle English word *whelmen* (to overturn), *whelm* has to do with a capsized boat, or a vessel turned upside down. From this thirteenth-century word did we create *overwhelm* as meaning "something completely covered over" (in the original case, with water).

Paparazzi

Any freelance photographer who aggressively pursues a celebrity for the purpose of obtaining that perfect candid shot is said to be a part of the paparazzi, but what exactly is paparazzi? Well, the word is Italian in origin and, literally translated, means "buzzing insects." (Anyone having seen the hoopla surrounding the better-known celebs of our time knows exactly where the word gets its meaning!)

Paying Through the Nose

To pay too much for something has long been the meaning behind "paying through the nose," though it can also mean paying in installments (which would, in most cases, *also* mean paying a higher price). The phrase is said to have originated in Sweden many years ago. At one time, the Swedish government charged a nose tax of one penny per person, which was basically nothing more than a head tax. Paying through the nose became synonymous with paying too much (which is not much different from what we feel about paying taxes today!).

Peanut Gallery

First you must know that peanuts are so named because they grow as peas in a pod. Similarly, the peanut gallery (that audience of people seated in the back of a theater) looks like a bunch of peas in a pod, from the performer's perspective onstage. The original peanut gallery referred to the cheap seats, second balcony up, in the theaters of the Gay Nineties. The name was coined not only from the appearance of the crowds, but also from the fact that the commoners in those seats were known to throw peanut shells at any actor or actress they particularly did not like.

Peeping Tom

In case you don't recall the story, Peeping Tom of Coventry, England, was the man who used a peephole to look at Lady Godiva as she rode through town, "... *clothed only in chastity.*" As the story has it, Tom was a tailor, and he was stricken with blindness for disobeying the order given all the townspeople not to look at the lady as she made her famous ride. (You might recall that Lady Godiva made her ride after begging her husband, Earl Leofric of Mercia, to take away an oppressive tax on the poor, which he said he would do if she would ride unclothed through town!)

Petticoat

Short for "petite coat," the original petticoat was designed for medieval warriors to wear under their armor to prevent chafing. It worked so well for the torso that soon length was added. As armor became more cumbersome than practical, it was the female population that saw a future for the petticoat as an undergarment for dresses and skirts.

Piggyback

Another word slurred over time! The correct word for carrying someone upon your back was *pick-a-back*, and it was first used to describe an adult carrying a child. *Pick-a-back* evolved to its current spelling and pronunciation today of "piggyback"!

Pig in a Poke

Buying a "pig in a poke" means you've bought something unseen, or that you've been scammed. The word *poke* in this case refers to a small sack or bag. From the French expression *"acheter chat en poche"* (or "buying a cat in a poke"), the reference made is to an old trick of substituting a cat for a baby pig. When someone, thinking he had purchased a pig at market, arrived home only to find a cat in his bag, the expression "letting the cat out of the bag" was born.

Pigtail

Now, how we got braids of hair out of a sow's behind took some maneuvering, but rest assured, the original pigtails *did* come from the farm! Aside from the authentic "tail of a pig," the next thing known as a pigtail was a pull of tobacco, twisted like a rope, which looked like a pig's tail. From this tobacco reference we concluded that braids of hair had the same ropelike appearance, and so we call them pigtails today.

Pin Money

When metal pins were first invented around the fourteenth century, they were quite costly and scarce. As a matter of fact, so precious were they that a law was decreed allowing women to purchase these pins only on January 1 and 2 of each year. For this purpose, men were known to give their wives money to purchase their yearly supply of pins. But when pins were no longer a monopoly and more readily come by, pin money became known as that money set aside for a woman to buy whatever niceties she might like from the allowance given her by her husband.

Pipe Down

To pipe down (or to "shut up," as one really means it) has a nautical beginning. "Pipe down!" was originally a command, from a ship's captain to his crew, to clear the decks and head below to safety. Once they'd done so, the ship was left silent and still (at least in appearance to other ships). Because of the instant results from the command, we use "Pipe down!" today to quickly quiet a crowd or a situation.

Pipe Dream

Many of our literary geniuses were known to have smoked a little opium in their day. (And most of them even inhaled!) Near the turn of the century, opiates were not seen as harmful but rather were viewed as "enhancers of creativity." First recorded by Wallace Irvin in 1901, a pipe dream was one influenced by the passing of the opium pipe.

Polecat

First off, a polecat is not a skunk. It is only found in Europe and is named for the animal it preyed upon, that being the *poule* (the French word for chicken, where we get our word *poultry* today). Skunks, on the other hand, *are* American, and can be differentiated from their European cousins by the distinguishing white stripe down the middle of their backs.

Powwow

We use *powwow* today to connote a meeting at which there is much talk, most often within a political context. The word, as you might imagine, comes from the Native American Indian and depicts the public feasts, dances, and gatherings of certain tribes. Today it is used loosely to signify any uproarious meeting at which there is more noise than deliberation, yet the original powwows were noisy celebrations that took place only *after* a successful war or hunt.

Quack

Those unprofessional MD's we might fondly refer to as quacks were originally known as quacksalvers. By definition and reputation, these were the cure-all medicine peddlers of the early sixteenth century, who quacked out the benefits of their salves and tonics as they traveled from town to town. These traveling medicine men were more often known for their entertainment styles than for their healing powers.

Quagmire

By definition, a quagmire is a surface that gives way when stepped on. We get the *quag* half of the term from the same root as *quake*. The *mire* is a marsh, or soft, muddy land. The word dates back to the mid-1500s and was coined to describe ground that appeared solid but in reality was unstable. Today we use the word to describe a similar feeling of uncertainty, or a sense of being "bogged down."

Quandary

That state of perplexity or doubt that we would call a quandary is believed to have originated some four centuries ago. An earlier phrase coined by the French, *"Qu'en dirai-je?"* is about the best explanation etymologists have come up with for this perplexing word. *"Qu'en dirai-je?"* was interpreted to mean "What shall I make of it?" And as that question is precisely what a person in a quandary would ask, it is believed that it is the basis for our word *quandary* today.

Quarantine

Quarantine, you might note, has the same prefix as the words *quadrant* and *quartet.* Created from the Italian *quaranta,* meaning "forty," the first quarantine dates back to the fourteenth century. Established as an attempt to protect coastal cities from the plague, quarantines were first practiced in Italian ports, when arriving ships were forced to sit at anchor for forty days before offloading their cargo.

Quarter Horse

As American as apple pie is the quarter horse. Yet, contrary to popular belief, the breed was not named for its lineage or size, but rather, the quarter horse was so named because of its ability to run high speeds in quarter-mile races. First named in 1834, the quarter horse is recognized as a breed unto itself, somewhat smaller than Thoroughbred racehorses, and characterized by its great endurance as well as its speed. The earliest quarter horses were also known as quarter nags.

(Cutting to the) Quick

The noun version of *quick* is that "sensitive or raw exposed flesh area, as under the fingernails." It came to us from the Anglo-Saxon word *cwicu*, meaning "alive or living." To cut to the quick means to cut through the outer covering (or flesh), diving straight to the sensitive, living matter within. In a more literary sense, "cutting to the quick" means tapping into the most personal and emotionally sensitive area of an issue at hand.

Quid Pro Quo

From Latin, *quid pro quo* specifically means "something for something," and that same "something" *(quid)* is the root word for Britain's pound sterling, used today. Originally, the phrase meant something (usually money) that was given in exchange for something else. While its first reference is unknown, Shakespeare used a similar expression in his *Henry VI* when he wrote, "I cry you mercy, 'tis but Quid for Quo."

Quintessential

The word we might use to describe the purest and most concentrated form of a thing was, in the beginning, designed to be a scientific explanation for things unseen. As medieval alchemists sought to find a fifth element to add to the existing earth, air, fire, and water, *quinta essentia,* or a "fifth essence," was theorized, and believed to be a form of ether. Studied as the substance of all heavenly bodies, this quintessence came to mean the most essential part or the primary material of any entity or idea.

Racking One's Brain

The torture treatment known as the rack was introduced into the Tower of London in the mid-1400s. Its name was derived from the German word *recken,* which meant "to stretch or draw out," and the punishment itself did just that. While this cruel and unusual torture treatment was banned in England less than two hundred years later, the phrase, with its image of one racking or stretching his brain, has remained a common figure of speech within the English language ever since.

Ragtime

That fun-loving music that's come to be known as ragtime is precisely what its name implies. At a time when most music was regimented and precise in rhythm (as were waltzes and traditional ballads), ragtime had no strict standard, and so was named literally for its ragged time. Known as the precursor of jazz, ragtime, with its syncopated melody and its accented accompaniment, became most popular around the turn of the century.

Raining Cats and Dogs

It was during the heaviest of rains back in seventeenth-century England that the remains of dogs and cats were often seen floating through the streets. The reason had to do with poor drainage systems and even poorer health-control laws. As these animals often drowned when there came a flood, it was soon said that it had "rained cats and dogs" (though at the time, the saying pertained more to polecats and dogs!).

Red-Letter Day

Not long after the calendar was created, it became the custom of monks and religious leaders to mark saints' days, holidays, and festivals in red ink. Because these days were usually festive and to be remembered, we carried the term red-letter day to its present meaning, which is *any* lucky or memorable day.

Red Tape

At one point in time, government documents were sealed with red ribbons, connoting their special nature and the special attention to be paid them. Because of the formality, the rules and procedures for both officials and lawyers in reviewing these papers, and the time consumed in those reviews (not to mention the time tying and untying ribbons), red tape became the symbol for the bureaucratic complexities that accompanied such papers.

Reimburse

Perhaps we all know that reimbursing has to do with paying someone back, or making restoration by way of payment for an equivalent sum of money, but the part you might *not* have known is just how literal the translation is. Derived from three Latin words, *re* means "back," *im* means "in," and *bursa* means "purse." So as we interpreted it, first from the Latin, and then from the French, *reimburse* meant to literally put the money back in another's purse. (If only they were all this easy!)

Riding
Roughshod

A roughshod horse was one whose shoes had nails protruding through. The concept was originally designed for horses on the battlefield, and the goal was to keep the animal from slipping. However, once on the battlefield, it was soon determined that roughshod horses not only held a better grip, but they were also able to do damage to any enemy that might have fallen in the fight. (Imagine the gory scene of one trampled by a roughshod horse! That same image will give you the meaning of "treating someone brutally" that we associate with the word *roughshod* today.)

Rings True

With the advent of gold and silver coins came the production of counterfeit money as well, and at one point in time, the only sure way to tell if a coin was solid was to drop it and listen for the tone it produced. It was said that a solid, true coin would "ring true," while a counterfeit one (filled with an alloy of nickel or copper) would sound flat. The test was known as ringing a coin, and it was later determined to be less than reliable. In any event, the practice led to the phrase "rings true" in connoting something that feels to be accurate.

Riot Act

Yes, Virginia, there really *was* a Riot Act! It was instigated by George I of England in 1715. At that time, in order to keep the peace, George made it against the law for twelve or more people to congregate at one time. Under this rule, if any public official encountered a crowd, he was required to read George's Riot Act, and if the people did not disperse, they were subject to a minimum of three years in prison.

Ritzy

When a person's name earns a word all its own, then it stands to reason that this was one impressive person! Such is true of Caesar Ritz, the Swiss restaurateur and hotel magnate who built the famous Ritz Hotel in Paris in 1898. Known for his strict standards of excellence, Ritz earned the reputation of being the greatest hotelier in all of the Western world. Once Ritz hotels were established in London, New York, and a handful of other prestigious cities, having something "like the Ritz," or "Ritzy," became the standard description for anything extravagant and lavish.

Rule of Thumb

As a rule of thumb, the rule is: That length between the last knuckle of the thumb and the thumb's tip is roughly an inch. So for early merchants and those selling ribbon, lace, or cloth, when an accurate measure wasn't readily available, the rule of thumb came into play. (Although the rule was an estimate, most everyone's thumb measured close to the same, so it was a safe bet to call on the rule when the situation required it!)

Rule the Roost

Granted, the cocky ways of a barnyard rooster certainly would fit the description of one who rules the roost, but the phrase is believed to reference something entirely different. In its original form, "rule the roost" was first recorded "rule the roast"! It came from old England and referred to the master of the house, who sat at the head of the table and served his guests. As ruler of the roast, that lord and master was responsible for both family and servants, and was indeed the authoritative figure of the household.

Rummage

Rummage, or "stir around," was originally the noun *roomage,* and was by definition "a storage place for cargo in a ship's hull." The verb came about as a result of searching that particular roomage place by handling, turning over, and/or disarranging. Picture the roomage of the ship, and you probably get a clearer idea of what *rummage* was intended to be!

Sabotage

Sabotage comes from the French *sabot*, meaning "wooden shoe," and it was the French who were the first saboteurs. When weaving looms were first introduced to the French during the Second World War, the workmen protested the loss of their jobs to machines by jamming their wooden shoes into the looms. From the destruction that came about from a wooden shoe, we get *sabotage* today.

Scapegoat

The original scapegoat was biblical in origin and is associated with the Jewish Day of Atonement, or Yom Kippur. In the sixteenth chapter of Leviticus, we are told that Aaron (the brother of Moses) was instructed to bring two goats to the door of the tabernacle. The scripture reads: "Aaron shall cast lots upon the two goats; one lot for the Lord, and the other lot for the scapegoat." The scapegoat was presented as the Lord's live offering and was allowed to go free, symbolically taking the sins of the people away into the wilderness. Today *scapegoat* is synonymous with one who takes the blame for another.

Scot-free

The word *scot*, from the Anglo-Saxon *sceot*, was a tax or a fine. The most common use of the word dates back to old England, where a "scot and lot" was a levy placed on all subjects according to their ability to pay. Now technically speaking, the first scot was a form of income tax. But today *scot-free* simply means getting off the hook without paying, be it taxes or otherwise.

Seventh Heaven

It is from the Islamic faith that we derive the phrase "seventh heaven." It is the Muslims' belief that there are seven levels of heaven, each progressively better than the previous one, each requiring a purer life to attain. According to Mohammed, the seventh heaven is formed of "divine light beyond the power of the tongue to describe." It is in this seventh heaven that pure bliss is found, as it is believed this is where God himself resides with his angels.

Shebang

We usually refer to the *whole* shebang when using this word, and by inference, we mean an entire lot or establishment. The word itself is believed to have come from the Irish word *shebeen,* which was an unlicensed or illegal drinking establishment of old. As this particular type of speakeasy was known for its brawls and fights, it was said that a drunken Irishman could often be heard challenging "the whole shebeen," and thus, the meaning for the word today.

Shoddy

While we use the word *shoddy* today to mean a product that is inferior in quality, it was originally a technical term used to describe a by-product that came from manufacturing wool. Some years ago, *shoddy* referred to the fluff part of weaving cloth that was thrown off in the spinning. While this fluff was still used to make new wool, it was short-stapled, which meant the clothes made from it did not last as long. As that fabric was inferior to the long-stapled or combing wools, it became known as shoddy, and hence our reference today.

Sidekick

A *kick* by definition in Old English was a pocket in the side of a man's trousers, not much different from a man's front pants pocket today (though somewhat deeper). Early pickpockets knew the difference between a kick and a pratt (the latter being the backside pocket). The kick was difficult to pick, as it was closest to the skin. Over time, a sidekick became known as a faithful friend who, just like a man's pocket, was ever by his side.

Silhouette

It was Étienne de Silhouette, the comptroller general of France in 1759, for whom these black-on-white pictures were named. History tells us that under Silhouette's administration, businesses were ordered, in the name of savings, to do away with all unnecessary details. By the same rule, even paintings were reduced to mere outlines. As a result, black-on-white portraits became popular, and were called silhouettes in honor of the financier whose economic plan had suggested them.

Skeleton
in the
Closet

Back in the Dark Ages it was long held by superstition that a doctor could not cut into the body of a dead person, for fear of disturbing its ghost. As a result, cadavers became hot items on the black market for doctors longing to study human anatomy. When grave robbers began to supply the goods, many a good doctor became suspected of having a skeleton in his closet, which gives us today's meaning of "private or hidden secrets."

Slapstick

Yes, there *is* an actual device called a slapstick, and as you might imagine, it originated with the vaudeville comedian. The slapstick was made of two flat pieces of wood, fastened at one end. When used by an actor to hit another person, the slapstick was known to make an unusually loud noise, and thus, it produced laughter when used in the vaudevillian's act. Back then, the slapstick was an actual prop. Today we use the word to sum up the horseplay and comedy that so often accompanies such sticks.

Slush Fund

The first slush fund was on a ship, and it came from the surplus of fat or grease from foods fried thereon. The crew of the boat was usually able to sell this "slush" in port, and the money was set aside for small luxuries. Currently the term refers to funds set aside from the regular funds or budgets needed to keep a business (or government) afloat, and has a connotation of being secretive and often corrupt.

Snob

The earliest colleges were never designed for the common man. Instead, they were made for nobility, those who would need an education to lead their country. Later, Cambridge University decided it would open its doors to more than just royalty, but entering students had to register as either "nobilitate" or "sine nobilitate" (without nobility). The latter was shortened to "S. nob" and is where we get our word *snob* today.

Son of a Gun

"Son of a gun" is nautical in origin. When women were allowed to accompany their husbands at sea, pregnancies soon followed, and it became common practice to give birth beneath the guns of a ship. Later, the term son of a gun was extended to include those conceived illegitimately aboard a ship, thus making something of a pun out of the more vulgar reference "son of a —."

Southpaw

Before the advent of nighttime baseball, games were played in the daylight, in the heat of the sun. Major league diamonds were, as a rule, laid out so that the batter would face east, opposite the setting sun, to spare his eyes the glare. Because of this configuration, the pitcher faced west, with his right hand to the north, and his left to the south. From this early baseball layout we coined the term southpaw for a left-handed pitcher.

Spats

Spats is merely the shortened word for spatterdashers, which were those protective coverings worn over shoes and ankles. While the looks of these coverings were somewhat dashing, they were originally designed for function, to protect a person's shoes and ankles from mud and rain, as it might spatter and splatter as they exited a carriage or cart.

Speakeasy

Earlier we referred to a speakeasy when describing "the whole shebang." Well, the Irish are to thank for this word, too, as it had to do with their prohibition laws of long ago. One was not allowed to raise one's voice riotously or start a brawl in any establishment where liquor was sold. To do so might call to the attention of the police the existence of the illegal establishment. The result was that patrons of such were to speak easy, both in the joint as well as about it. Today speakeasies are simply known as places where illegal alcohol is sold.

Spittin' Image

This phrase is a corruption of "spirit and image," which was coined by early Americans to describe a relative (usually a child) who both looked and had the disposition of another family member. The phrase was used so regularly that in the South it was phonetically contracted to "spittin' image," while holding on to its basic premise of "just like another."

Stooge

You'll have to go back to the days of early theater to find the original stooges. They were, quite simply, stool pigeons, or those people planted in an audience to bear the brunt of the vaudeville comedian's jokes. Because their real identity was not known to the audience, they were referred to as stool pigeons, which was later shortened to *stooge* (the "stage/stool pigeon").

Taking the Cake

This expression was inspired by the gatherings by the slave population on early Southern plantations, where cakewalks were a sort of dance competition. In such, various participants "strutted their stuff," in order to take the cake as a prize. We've since carried the cakewalk tradition over to our county fairs and festivals today, though "taking the cake" now represents something unusual or unbelievable.

Talking Turkey

History has it that the first turkey talk went something like this: After a day of hunting, an early American settler and an Indian were dividing their spoils of three crows and two wild turkeys. The settler gave the Indian the first bird, a crow, as he took for himself a turkey. Next he gave the Indian another crow, and took for himself the second turkey. Upon giving the Indian the third crow, the Indian objected, and the settler pointed out that the Indian was given three birds to his two, to which the Indian replied, *"We stop talk birds, we now talk turkey."*

Thimble

Sometimes our word origins are just downright practical, and *thimble* definitely falls into this category. The thimble was invented  to protect the thumb of the seamstress or quilter, back when all sewing was done by hand. Originally, it was called a thumb-bell, obviously because of its shape, and its purpose in protecting the thumb.

Third Degree

The Freemasons gave us this expression, and while much of what they do is in secret, it is said that the third degree is the highest one can obtain in becoming a Master Mason. But to do so, one must undergo the most difficult of proficiency testing, and it is from these tests that we borrow the phrase to connote the exhaustive questioning most often identified with police in their attempts to solve a case.

Three Sheets to the Wind

True, the origin of this one is nautical, but *no,* the sheets are not the sails! The sheets being referred to here are the ropes attached to the corners of the sails, which are used for lowering or extending. When all three sheets (on a vessel with three sails) are loosened, the ship will rock and reel as though without course or purpose, much like a drunk would if walking about while intoxicated.

Threshold

Farmhouses of old had nothing but earth for floors, so for covering, leftover threshings from the fall harvest were often scattered on the floor to serve as insulation against the cold ground. To keep the threshings at the entrance from blowing out every time a door was opened, stone or wooden thresholds were invented to hold the loose trappings in place. Today the threshold refers simply to the entrance itself.

Tinker's Dam

No, this dam had nothing to do with profanity; rather, it had to do with something of very little value. A tinker's dam was a dam made of dough or clay that was used to confine the molten solder of a pot or pan in repair. As its purpose was solely to keep the solder from spreading where it was not needed, once it had served its usefulness, the tinker's dam was discarded. As a result of this frequently used and virtually worthless solution, a tinker's dam has become universally synonymous with something worth nothing.

Tip

Now, there are a lot of questions about the practice of tipping, but it helps to know the origin of the term in order to truly understand the concept. TIP is an acronym standing for "to insure promptness." The practice was started years ago in English inns and taverns as a means of motivating the poorly paid help to get a move on, and take care of their customers in a more timely and professional manner.

True Blue

The origin of "true blue" as it pertains to one who is totally honest, faithful, and dependable has more than one history. The first, they say, had to do with the fast-dyeing qualities of the English color Coventry blue. Now, whether it was actually Coventry blue or not, blue was adopted as the official color of the pro-Parliament Scottish Presbyterian party in seventeenth-century England. As this color was chosen to be a direct contradistinction to the royal red of the Royalist Party, those said to be true blue were considered to be among the loyalists and the faithful.

True Colors

The original true colors were shown in the flags of early sailing ships. Pirate legend has it that many a good ship was conned into believing it was approaching the ship of a friendly nation because of the flag it flew. However, once the ships were within cannon shot of each other, the pirate vessel quickly changed its flag, showing its true colors, just before looting its victims.

Turncoat

You have to go back in history just a bit to find the first turncoats. Truth is, they date back to the days of feudal lords, each of whom maintained his own individual army. Each lord also had his own insignia, and when a servant left one lord for the service of another's army, he was said to have turned his coat inside out, so as not to be mistaken for the enemy.

Two Bits

As we know from "two bits, four bits, six bits . . . a dollar," a couple of bits must be worth about a quarter. Originally, our dollar was based on the Spanish dollar, which could easily be divided into eight parts (hence, "pieces of eight"). In the West Indies, where Spanish money was widely used, paper dollars were at one time cut up into eight parts, with each being referred to as a "bit." As one bit was equal to twelve and a half cents, two bits were the equivalent of a quarter today—obviously a sum not worth very much; thus, our reference to something pretty cheap!

Tycoon

Think of a tycoon and you probably envision one of great wealth and power. Truth is, the Japanese gave us the word; it comes from *tai,* meaning "great," and *kun,* which means "prince." The interesting part is that the Japanese did not use the word among their own but rather only when speaking to foreigners in attempts to impress them with their own importance. It was Commodore Perry who brought the word back from Japan in the mid-1850s. We've been using it ever since to describe our own shoguns.

Umble Pie

True, we use the phrase as though it means humble, but the original word was *umble*. Umbles (in case you didn't know) are the entrails of a deer. Long ago, when hunters would prepare the venison from a hunt, the insides or entrails were saved and prepared in a pie for the servants to eat. As these servants obviously humbled themselves to eat the less desirable portions, "eating umble pie" became the pun, and stood as a symbol for one who subordinates himself to another.

Umpire

From the Old French *non per,* meaning "not equal," the original umpire was a third person called in to settle an argument. As this person was the deciding vote in the matter, he was said to have been "not paired," or a "non peer" to the situation. For whichever reference you choose, the umpire was hired to be an impartial third party.

Uncle Sam

Historically, the original Uncle Sam was one Samuel Wilson, co-owner of a slaughterhouse in Troy, New York, that was responsible for selling pork and beef to the U.S. Army during the War of 1812. The meat sold to the U.S. government by Sam and his uncle, Elbert Anderson, was stamped "E.A.–U.S." (for "Elbert Anderson–United States"). Story has it that a soldier once asked what the initials stood for and was told, "Elbert Anderson's uncle Sam," after which the "Uncle Sam" part soon spread as the national nickname for the U.S. government.

Under the Weather

Again, to find this origin, we must return to the high seas and the lingo of the sailors there. Any greenhorn aboard a ship, subject to the nausea of seasickness, was encouraged to go below the decks, or under the weather, where the motions of the wind and the waves were minimal, and would not make worse an already sickening situation.

Up a Creek

This one has several variations, including "up Salt Creek" and "up a creek without a paddle." There's even the euphemism that we won't go into here. In any event, "up a creek" refers to being in a bad predicament, and the expression dates back some hundred years. Originally, it *was* Salt Creek that one was up, when he was in a tight spot. Salt creeks, by definition, are those waterways leading through marshes or stagnant waters as rivers open to the ocean. Owing to the thickening scum factor of the interchanging waters, a boatman without a paddle would be stuck for sure. It is believed the phrase was popularized in an 1884 political campaign song entitled "Blaine up Salt Creek."

Upper Crust

In the mid-1400s it was societally proper to serve kings and royalty the upper half of a loaf of bread, while saving the scraps and crumbs for the lowly servants. As only the rich and powerful were allowed to eat the upper crust, the expression soon became synonymous with those of rank and importance.

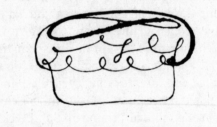

Upper Hand

Some believe the "upper hand" has to do with the age-old game wherein two individuals place hand over hand along a stick or bat until one reaches the top. Obviously, according to the rules of this common game, the upper hand is the winner. However, the phrase predates the invention of this game by some two hundred years. It is believed that "upper hand," used to connote authority or seniority, came from the now-obsolete "over hand," which was the term used to mean one having mastery or control over another.

Upstage

Those familiar with the theater know that upstage is to the rear of the boards, while downstage is up front. But what you may not know is that stages of old raised their upstages in order to make actors there appear higher and taller than the other actors to the stage's front. Today we use the word out of theatrical context to refer to anyone who attempts to outshine another.

Up to Snuff

A couple of theories exist on the origin of this phrase, the first being that *snuff* is really a derivative of *sniff*. As smell is the most sensitive of all our senses, being up to sniff meant all senses were intact (i.e., one is feeling fine!). The second theory has to do with tobacco. As snuff has long been the cheapest form of the product and more easily come by than cigars or cigarettes, one not up to snuff was one who was flat broke indeed! Whether one is broke or one's olfactory isn't on par, "up to snuff" is still synonymous today with a certain standard of well-being.

Utopia

It was Sir Thomas More in 1516 who gave us *Utopia*, though few, perhaps, know how he came by the name. Sir Thomas named his imaginary island of perfection using the Greek words *ou* ("not") and *topos* ("a place"). Put them together and you have a visionary heaven that is, in reality, "no place" on earth. *Utopia* had such an impact on the literary world that its title soon became a word unto itself, meaning "ideal."

Vandal

Vandals today destroy, damage, and deface property, and the original Vandals did much the same. A tribe of some eighty thousand living around A.D. 450, the first Vandals may best be remembered for sacking Rome, and later persecuting early Christians. As they were responsible for destroying many valuable cultural objects along the way, the word *vandalism* now signifies wanton destruction, especially as it pertains to fine art. Technically the word *vandal* means "wanderer," as the tribe was known for its wandering conquests throughout France, Spain, and Africa.

Varsity

The word *varsity,* which stands for a "principal team representing a college or university," is simply the shortened version of *university.* It started in England, with Oxford and Cambridge, and was originally written *versity,* although it was pronounced the way we spell it today.

Vaudeville

That wonderful form of stage entertainment known as vaudeville was named for the place of its origin, vau-de-Vire, which is located in the northwest part of France. Vire was both a river and a town in Normandy, which became famous for its unique form of theatrics, as well as for its songs and short plays. Translated "valley of the Vire," vaudeville soon became synonymous with the pantomimes, dancing, skits, and songs associated therewith.

Ventriloquist

Once thought to be associated with witch-craft, ventriloquism has to do with that unique talent of producing a voice that appears to be coming from some place other than the speaker's mouth. Originally, that sound was thought to be coming from the stomach, hence the name ventriloquist, from the Latin *ventri,* meaning "belly," and *loqui,* meaning "to speak." The first ventriloquists were said to be those who "spoke from their bellies." Later, the art was improved to the point that the sound seemed to be coming from such places as a dummy or a corner of a room.

Verdict

Today's word describing a jury's decision at the end of a trial is one that dates back to the Middle Ages. With the introduction of the jury, it was superstitiously believed that twelve men in a group would hold some mystical power in drawing a truthful conclusion. (The number twelve was considered holy both in reference to the twelve tribes of Israel and Jesus' twelve apostles.) It was the French who gave this body of twelve the name of *veir* ("true") and *dit* ("said"). Even in homicide cases today, a verdict cannot be obtained until all twelve on the jury reach an agreement.

Veto

One powerful little word is *veto*! With four little letters, the head of state has the power to cancel out laws passed by lower governing bodies. The word comes directly from Latin, its translation literally "I forbid." It was used in a political context as far back as the time of the Roman senate, and has carried the same meaning both within and without political circles for hundreds of years.

Visa

Short for the Latin phrase *carta visa*, a visa is that official authorization that permits entry into another country. The original phrase means "papers seen," which was the stamp of approval by those on border control, monitoring the visitors coming in and out of a foreign country.

Vodka

Distilled from a mash of rye, barley, or even potatoes, vodka was invented by the Russians and named by them as well. While its name was derived from the Russian word *voda*, meaning "water," vodka was not originally named such because of its waterlike appearance. Rather, it was so named because at the time of its invention, it was believed that the spirits of vodka were as essential to life as water itself! (Incidentally, *whiskey* shares a similar history, hailing from the Gaelic *uisge beatha*, meaning "water of life.")

Volume

Ancient texts were written on sheets of paper scrolled around large sticks and fastened together lengthwise for easy storage. *Volume* we take from the Latin word *volvere,* which means simply "to roll." Because these were our earliest books, the English adopted *volume* to mean "one of a collection of books comprising a whole set."

Wall Street

The literal and figurative symbol of all things financial, Wall Street is located in downtown Manhattan and takes its name from a wall that stretched the entire length of the current street when the Dutch first settled in the area. Since the early nineteenth century, Wall Street has become synonymous with the American economy, and to this day we fondly remember the street, owing to a simple wall that once stood in its place.

Wearing Your Heart on Your Sleeve

Wearing your heart on your sleeve was customary among knights at one time. In reality, the actual heart worn was a scarf or handkerchief given by a damsel to her knight, prior to his going off to fight. The scarf, worn by the knight as an armband, was a symbol to his fellow soldiers that his body might be in battle, but his heart was somewhere else.

Wet Behind the Ears

Refer to one who is naive, immature, anything less than wise in the ways of the world, and you're talking "wet behind the ears." As the image might suggest, this wetness has to do with the likes of a newborn, be it a human, a lamb, or a colt. As the last place to dry on a newborn is that small place behind the ears, the phrase connotes the innocence of one just starting to make his way in the world, but who is still feeling the safety of his first surroundings.

Whipping Boy

Some trace this to King Edward VI (the feeble son of England's Henry VIII), others to James I (the young prince who became Charles I). In any event it was decided by the royal family that, as royal heirs were so sacred (and many of them teetering in health), an elected peer, equivalent in age to young would-be kings, should be the recipient of any punishments on behalf of the royal prince. Today we use "whipping boy" to connote anyone punished for the mistakes of another, especially when a worker takes the heat for a superior.

White Collar/ Blue Collar

The phrases we now use to describe differences in workforce classes date back to the early 1920s. The white collars were those who performed nonmanual labor (or duties not requiring work clothes) and included office workers and those who had not joined unions. Blue collars referred to those who worked with their hands, most often for an hourly wage, most often in unions. Interestingly enough, the counterparts to white collars and blue collars in England are black coats and hard hats, respectively; again, so named for the types of jobs the worker performs.

White Elephant

In Siam, it was once law that if the rare albino elephant was trapped, it was to be given to the emperor. While the motive of saving this endangered breed was noble, the task of maintaining such a creature was difficult. With each elephant came the selection of someone to keep the sacred pet, and that gift, because of its expense and trouble, was one *no one* hoped to receive.

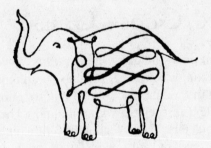

Whole Nine Yards

It's understandable that you might think the nine yards referred to here is some form of material, but it isn't. Truth of the matter is, the "whole nine yards" refers to the maximum amount of cement the original cement trucks could hold. It was the construction industry that gave us the "whole nine yards," as their standard cement trucks could carry enough mix for nine cubic yards of concrete per load.

Wild Goose Chase

To be sent on a wild goose chase means to waste time pursuing a thing that perhaps doesn't merit pursuing in the first place. According to sources, the problems associated with wild goose chases are twofold. First, the wild goose is a difficult bird to catch, and second, even if you catch one, there's not much you can do with a wild goose! Therefore, to send a person on a wild goose chase means you've put him in pursuit of something not very practical, and at best, it's not worth the energy expended if successful.

(Sowing One's) Wild Oats

Most know "sowing wild oats" has to do with giving up one's youthful, wild, and often immature ways, but Scandinavian folklore gives a fuller meaning. According to legend, thick fogs and vapors would rise from the earth just before the land would blossom into vegetation. In Denmark they referred to these vapors as *Lokkens havre*, which translates "Loki's wild oats"! As the god of strife and evil in Norse mythology, Loki was believed to transform himself into one last mystical mist before settling down to a season of productive harvests.

Windfall

While we use the word *windfall* today to mean "any good fortune or gain that befalls us," the term originated in medieval England, where it was then against the law for commoners to cut down a tree. However, if the wind blew down a branch or knocked over a tree, the firewood became fair game, available to anyone who picked it up, so the earliest windfalls were good fortune, indeed.

Win, Place, or Show

Granted, most folks know that the origin of "win, place, or show" dates back to the earliest racetracks. But most may not know that the phrase was so named because of the way in which the finishes were announced. As small boards were used to record the names of the winners of each horse race, and as these boards were *so* small that only the first two could be "placed" on the board, the titles "win" and "place" were soon coined. Shortly after, a second board was used to "show" the third winner, and "win, place, or show" became synonymous with first, second, and third!

X (for a Kiss!)

The original X used to designate a kiss dates back to medieval times, and believe it or not, it was a legal custom. In attempts to show good faith, the X (symbol for Saint Andrew) was placed after each signature on papers of importance. To further reinforce the pledge made in the documents, the signee was required to kiss the X as a guarantee of his or her obligation. Over time, the association with the legal profession has been long forgotten, but the X we still remember as the sign for a kiss.

Xmas

While some consider it disrespectful to substitute an X for the *Christ* part of *Christmas*, others know that the letter X was in fact the symbol used long ago for Christ. X represents the Greek letter *chi*, which is the initial letter of the Greek word for Christ. And according to first-century history, the early Greek Christians used the letter X to stand for Christ, much as they used the fish with the X in the tail to represent Jesus.

X-ray

The X-ray was discovered by Nobel prize–winning physicist Wilhelm Conrad Röntgen and is called the "Röntgen Ray" by those in the field today. Röntgen, himself, called his discovery the X-ray, borrowing the *X* from the algebraic symbol for the unknown. His discovery was purely accidental, and at the time, difficult for him to comprehend; hence his reference to the unknown, or *X* factor.

XXX

Believe it or not, the triple-*X* mark connoting liquor or brew actually had a functional purpose in its original context. Dating back to the British brewers of the nineteenth century, bottlers labeled their brew for potency. One *X* was the weakest proof, while three *X*'s meant the stuff was pretty stout (and was the most common). It was our moonshiners during American Prohibition who borrowed the symbol *XXX* to brand their whiskey.

Xylophone

From the Greek words *xylo,* meaning "wooden," and *phone,* meaning "sound," the first xylophone was an invention of a native African, and it was used for chasing away evil spirits. Later, the wooden sounds became a common form of entertainment, and later yet, the idea of adding tubular resonators under the bars to increase the sound gave birth to the marimba. From the marimba, a keyboard was later added, giving us the celesta (the French word for "heavenly").

Yahoo

Perhaps you think of yahoos as bumpkins or hicks, but their true identity is really much worse. The Yahoos, as they were first described, were just a notch above barbaric beasts. Yahoos came from Jonathan Swift's famous *Gulliver's Travels*. It was in his fourth and last voyage that Gulliver traveled to the land of the educated horses, the Houyhnhnms, who held as slaves the nasty, human animals called *Yahoos*. According to Swift's depiction, the Yahoos were the worst that could be found in all mankind, and so goes the meaning we associate with it today.

Yankee

While there are several theories on the origin of *Yankee*, the most popular is that it's a derivation from the Dutch nickname "Jan Kee" (or "John Cheese"). As Holland was known for its cheese, the pejorative term was first used by British sailors in reference to Dutch freebooters. As the Dutch first settled in New York, *Yankee* became quite common as a derogatory nickname, usually preceded by a *damn*.

(Spinning a) Yarn

To "spin a yarn," as it refers to telling a tale, is originally naval talk that dates back to the early nineteenth century. It is believed that the yarn here has to do with the yarn lofts of old, wherein yarn was spun to supply the ships with rope. As the interweaving of the threads and the spinning of the twine took much time in developing rope, so, too, was the case in telling a really good story. Add to that the obvious pastime of gossip that most often accompanied the task of yarn weaving, and you've spun a good yarn while telling a really juicy tale!

Ye

While it sounds like a British version of *you*, the *ye* from the Old Country was in actuality a symbol called a thorn, and it represented the sound *th*. Originally, the Anglo-Saxon letter looked more like a *P*, but sloppy sign painters over time made the symbol look more like a *Y*. In its day, however, the word *ye* was always pronounced *the*, just as we would today.

Yellow Journalism

Yellow has held an association with the print medium for several hundred years, ever since certain tabloidesque books and newspapers were known by their cheap yellow coverings. The term "yellow journalism," however, was first coined in 1898 as "Yellow Kid Journalism," in reference to a series of cartoons that ran in William Randolph Hearst's New York *Journal.* As Hearst's paper took on Joseph Pulitzer's highly circulated New York *World,* sensationalized war reporting between the two competing papers netted us both the cartoon and the term meaning "borderline journalism," as we know it today.

Yen for

Some will say the reference to yen as a craving or desire is a derivation of *yearning,* but the word makes much more sense when you know that the Old Chinese word *yen* meant opium. From that context, having a yen for something meant far more than a craving. Rather, it was more like an addiction. The Japanese word *yen,* we believe, came from the Chinese word *yuan*, meaning a circular object, hence, a coin.

Yokel

The original yokels were woodpeckers in the Old Country, named for the sounds they made. In England today, *yokels* refer to those who live in the country (or where the yokels live!), and we've borrowed their term over time. (It's interesting to note that the reference to yokels as country folk is no different from our own reference to blue jays in the early days of this country. See *Jaywalker.*)

Yule

By translation, *Yule* is Norse for "jolly," and such was the mood at Yuletime festivals of old. Originally a heathen holiday, later changed by Catholic priests into a Christian event, the celebration of Yule kicked off the winter solstice. At the time of this shortest day of the year, a twelve-day feast was held, marked by the burning of the lighted Yule log and the singing of carols. Today we have the twelve days of Christmas as a salute to the feast of the Yule, and we sing Yuletide carols in celebration!

Zest

Leave it to the French to name the peel of a lemon or orange for the kick it added to food and drink! Dating back to the seventeenth century, the word *zest* was derived from the Latin word *scistus*, meaning "cut." By taking this cut of citrus and adding it to everything from basic water to fine cuisine, the French created both a flavorful (zesty) addition for their sense of taste, and a creative new word for their colorful vocabulary!

Zinger

Yes, those pointed little remarks made to "zing" another actually had an origin! The namesake is one John Peter Zenger, who in 1735 served time for his outspoken political barbs made in the New York *Weekly Journal*. As William Cosby, Colonial governor of New York at the time, was the primary recipient of these remarks (and as Cosby was less than happy about the bad press), Zenger was jailed for eight months without a trial for seditious libel. Though later acquitted by a jury, Zenger is remembered today for the barbing technique he made famous!

ZIP Code

We refer to it every day, but how many of us know that the *ZIP* stands for "Zone Improvement Program"? Okay, so you may have known that, but do you know what the five-digit code represents? Well, according to our reliable postal people, the first three digits indicate a district, usually a city, while the remaining two digits correspond with a local zone.

Zipper

Named for the *zipping* sound it makes, the word *zipper* was trademarked by B. F. Goodrich in 1925 for the fastening device for a new line of waterproof overshoes—kind of a rubber-coated boot. As the zipper technology was quick to catch on, the term soon became popular as a fastener for a number of applications, and Goodrich lost their zipper trademark for everything but their original boots.

ABOUT THE AUTHOR

KARLEN EVINS is producer and cohost of *Beyond Reason*, a nationally syndicated radio talk show dealing in spirituality and the unknown. She has worked as a television weather anchor, commentator, and as cohost of Nashville's longest-running morning-drive radio show for the past twenty years. She successfully self-published *I Didn't Know That* as two volumes in the early 1990s and currently writes a syndicated column by the same name. Karlen is a lifelong Tennessee resident, living in Nashville with her two dogs, Ike and Minsky.